Michigan Memories: True Stories From Two Peninsulas' Past

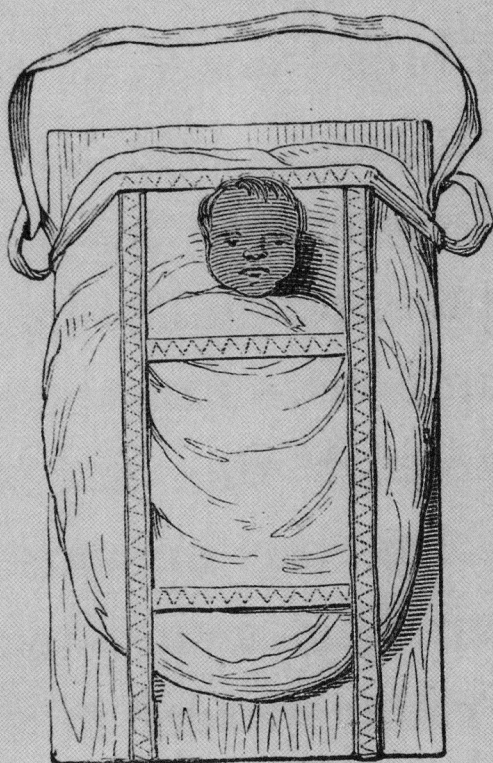

A Papoose.

Voyageurs and Indian women trip the light fantastic toe at a North Country ball in the 1850s.

Also By Larry B. Massie

Birchbark Belles (1993)
Potawatomi Tears & Petticoat Pioneers (1992)
The Romance of Michigan's Past (1991)
Pig Boats & River Hogs (1990)
Copper Trails & Iron Rails (1989)
Voyages Into Michigan's Past (1988)
Warm Friends & Wooden Shoes (1988)
From Frontier Folk to Factory Smoke (1987)
     with Priscilla Massie
Walnut Pickles & Watermelon Cake (1990)
     with Peter Schmitt
Battle Creek: The Place Behind the Product (1984)
Kalamazoo: The Place Behind the Product (1981)

Michigan Memories: True Stories From Two Peninsulas' Past

by
Larry B. Massie

The Priscilla Press
Allegan Forest, Michigan
1994

Copyright 1994 by Larry B. Massie

Please direct any questions or comments concerning this publication to: Larry B. Massie, 2109 41st St. Allegan Forest, MI. 49010 (616) 673-3633

Cover by Judi Miller Morris
Title Graphic by Devon Blackwood
Printing by Bookcrafters, Chelsea, MI.
Photographic Processing by Loren McKinstry

The cover art work, a water color executed by Allegan artist Judi Miller Morris, depicts a scene from "Drama in the Dunes," chapter one of this book.

ISBN: Soft Cover 1-886167-00-1
       Hard Cover 1-886167-01-X

First Edition   - October 1994

For Thomas G. Massie, my brother and my friend.

TABLE OF CONTENTS

Preface

To know Michigan is to love her. And like a happy marriage, each day spent together strengthens that love, binds it more firmly with shared memories. I cherish those Michigan experiences that have been imprinted on my soul.

The seasons assail the senses: crisp spring mornings with a whiff of wood smoke curling from the chimney and a cacophony of bird voices - gold finches, nut hatches, cardinals, evening grosbeaks and friendly chickadees - the tingle all over of the first swim at Littlejohn Lake in May, the bath warm surf at South Haven in July, the awesome fury of storm lashed Lake Superior in October - the incomparable taste of asparagus tips snapped an hour before in an overgrown field, of elusive morels, raspberries, little wild strawberries, big thimble-like blackberries and sweet corn dripping with butter - the over ripe smell of the fall, great vees of honking geese heading north and winding dirt roads ablaze with scarlet maples, rusty oaks and banana yellow sassafras.

I will never forget the satisfaction of catching my breath while viewing Lake Michigan after climbing the stairs at Saugatuck's Mt. Baldy - the reckless abandon of plunging in giant strides down the log slide near Grand Marais - the tinkle of ice shards jostling each other in the current as I glide on skies along the Kalamazoo River's banks.

I revel in the thrill of discovery: the sharp edge of a perfect flint arrowhead scooped from the sand and squeezed in my palm - ancient pine stump fences angling through the woods, half-century old initials carved on the muscular blue skin of a solitary beech tree, the hushed majesty of the forest elders at Hartwick Pines - that first encounter with the Italianate facades lining the quaint streets of many a village off the beaten path, the finding of a log-marked butt cut long ago by a timber pirate on the St. Marys River, - the fragrance of worn leather and vanilla like paper in a newly encountered old book shop in Niles or Marquette and the heart throbbing thrill of finding a long sought volume priced cheaply.

Dear to my heart is the romance of abandoned lighthouses, ferry rides to Mackinac, Beaver, Drummond and Sugar islands and that first glimpse from the south of the magnificent Mackinac Bridge no matter how many times I have seen it before.

Yes, Michigan leaves its mark on all who come here. Over the centuries, many have preserved their memories of the peninsulas and those records survive as a heritage that makes our individual recollections all the more meaningful and precious.

In this volume I have assembled a witch's brew of indelible memories: fur traders watching the drama of an Ottawa trial held amid the tawny Grand Haven dunes - colorful voyageurs ladling steaming stew then sleeping beneath overturned birch bark bateaux beside the lapping Great Lakes - the recollections of three centuries of visitors to the fairy isle the Indians called the Great Turtle - corset making women wearily weaving those instruments of torture, foundrymen fashioning stoves that once warmed the nation and patent medicine hucksters compounding alcohol-laden potions - town founders listening for the train whistle that will determine their community's destiny - literary lumberjacks with sawdust in their hair and ink in their veins - Gen. Custer in Monroe, a Scot who saw the Sault in 1854, the saga of the "Sage of East Aurora" and more. I hope you enjoy these true stories of our two peninsulas' past.

Larry B. Massie
Allegan Forest

Drama In The Dunes

Slowly, solemnly, head held high and face expressionless, the Indian advanced to where the Ottawa chief awaited him. His wife and children followed in single file. As he walked the brave thumped a drum in a monotonous beat and he chanted his death song.

Stopping within a pace of the chief, he laid the drum on the sand while his family took their places on the mats that had been spread for them. Then, looking the chief square in the eyes, he pulled a knife from his belt and said: "I, in a drunken moment, stabbed your son, being provoked to it by his accusing me of being a coward and calling me an old woman. I fled to the marshes at the head of the Muskegon, hoping that the Great Spirit would favor me in the hunt, so that I could pay you for your lost son. I was not successful. Here is the knife with which I killed your son; by it I wish to die. Save my wife and children. I am done."

Taking the knife, the chief handed it to his oldest son who stood behind him and grunted simply, "Kill him!"

The son stepped forward and laying one hand on the man's shoulder he looked directly into his eyes, trying to detect any sign of fear. He saw none - the Indian returned his gaze stoically, calmly - to show fear in the face of death was to loose your honor, forever, that was the Ottawa way.

Suddenly the chief's son jerked the knife forward as if to stab him and still the brave moved not a muscle. The executioner made another feint and another - the man stood emotionless, awaiting justice.

It was a beautiful May morning in 1819. From the tops of the surrounding sand dunes that rear their great tawny flanks at the mouth of the Grand River, the future site of Grand Haven, hundreds of Ottawa

13

looked down at the drama unfolding below.

Among those who observed the Indian trial from the sandy heights was Gurdon Hubbard, one of a brigade of American Fur Company voyageurs en route to their annual rendezvous at Mackinac Island, then the hub of a gigantic fur trading network that stretched to the Mississippi River and beyond. Though but 18 at the time, Hubbard had already developed the powerful physique and endurance that enabled him to travel up to 75 miles a day on foot. In recognition of his prowess the Indians named him Pa-Pa-Ma-Ta-Be, the swift walker. Destined to play an important role in the subsequent development of Chicago, Hubbard also plied his pen with noteworthy skill in describing in picturesque detail the action packed story of his early life as a fur trader. The pages of the autobiography published two years after his death in 1886, preserve some of the choicest accounts of Michigan during the colorful era when "beaver was king."

Born in Windsor, Vermont, on August 22, 1802, Hubbard moved with his family to Montreal at the age of 13. His father, a lawyer who had lost his fortune to unwise speculation, sought to better his lot in Canada. But on reaching Montreal, he discovered that the terms of a new law prohibited him from practicing his profession until he had resided in the dominion for five years. Continuing poverty brought an end to the young Hubbard's formal education and he worked at a succession of low paying jobs to bolster the family finances.

Eager for adventure, like many a teenager, the 15-year-old secured a position as a clerk with the American Fur Company through the recommendation of a friend. He signed on at an annual salary of $120 for a five year stint with the company founded by wealthy New York entrepreneur John Jacob Astor.

Embarking from Montreal on May 13, 1818, as

In an era when "beaver was king" Indian trading posts were
sometimes social centers.

part of a fleet of bateaux heavily laden with trade goods and rowed by singing French Canadian voyageurs, Hubbard made the arduous seven week journey to Mackinac Island. They paddled and pulled from shore up the rapids filled St. Lawrence River, along Lake Ontario to Toronto and then via portages and streams to Lake Huron. When he reached the island Hubbard reported to resident manager Ramsay Crooks. Sizing up the "still wet behind the ears" clerk Crooks determined to test his mettle by assigning him to the tedious and back breaking task of sorting furs. All that summer Hubbard labored from 5 a.m. to 7 p.m., with but an hour off for lunch, grading, counting and pressing into bales the thousands of pelts that flowed to the island in birch bark bateaux.

Hubbard proved himself by sticking it out through that miserable summer's work. Crooks then teamed him up with an experienced French trader named Deschamps, the leader of a trading brigade bound for the Illinois Country. They left Mackinac Island in September and paddled south along the east coast of Lake Michigan. At the future site of Ludington, Hubbard observed the cedar cross erected over the grave of Father Jacques Marquette in 1675. He spent the winter at various trading posts situated on the Illinois, Wabash and Mississippi rivers.

In late March, 1819, the voyageurs heaped their canoes with great glistening bales of beaver and other prize pelts and began their return journey to Mackinac Island. En route they tarried for several days at Chicago and at the mouth of the St. Joseph River so that they would be on hand to witness the Ottawa Feast of the Dead at the Grand River.

A funeral custom long practiced by the Iroquoian and Algonquian tribes of the Great Lakes; including the "Brothers of the Three Fires," the Potawatomi, Ottawa and Chippewa who peopled

Michigan, the Feast of the Dead was traditionally held at three to 12 year intervals. When the time arrived the bodies of tribal members who had died during the intervening years were retrieved from temporary burial scaffolds or disinterred from graves. It then befell the women relatives the task of tenderly and lovingly stripping the remaining flesh from the corpses until nothing but polished bones remained. Packed in birch bark mococks, the bones were conveyed to the designated site of the Feast of the Dead - a week long celebration filled with orations, feasting, and games. The climax of the ritual came with a mass burial of the bones along with artifacts intended to be of value to the spirits of the departed. Then and only then were those spirits finally free to make their journey to the next world.

While commandant at Fort Michilimackinac, near present day Mackinaw City, in 1694-99, Detroit's founder, Antoine de la Mothe Cadillac, had witnessed a Feast of the Dead conducted by some resident Huron and Ottawa. He wrote:

They erect a hut about 120 feet long, with new bark which never has been used before. They set up a maypole at each end and another in the middle, taller than the others. These poles are oiled, greased, and painted; at the top of each is a prize, which belongs to the person who can first reach it and touch it with his hand. They then enter this new hut, in which there are several tiers, and bring the bones of their relatives, in small bags or wrapped very neatly in strips of bark. They set them out then, from one end to the other, and heap gifts upon them of all their finest and best possessions, and generally whatever they have got together in the previous three years. Meanwhile, the cooking pots are constantly on the fire, full of meat, for anyone to eat who likes.

The Feast of the Dead as pictured in P. Lafitau's 1724 book
about Indian life.

They make a continual noise, night and day, with drums or by striking the pots or the strips of bark with sticks. They go out from time to time and surround the hut, firing muskets and howling until the whole air quivers; then they re-enter, bedaubed with black. Finally, the same tumult goes on for three days and three nights; but, before the time has quite expired, they make presents to those who have been invited to the feast of all that belongs to the dead, that is, of all the booty with which the bones were covered. When this has been distributed they go out for the last time and surround the hut, uttering great howls; they fall upon it with heavy blows with sticks and poles, making a desperate clatter, and break all the bark in pieces. When that is done, the women are ready with faggots of fir-branches, and they put a layer of them on the ground from one end to the other of the place where the hut was.

At the same time they kill a large number of dogs, which are to them what sheep are to us, and are valued by them more than any other animal, and make a feast of them. But, before eating, they set up two great poles and fasten a dog to the top of them, which they sacrifice to the sun and the moon, praying to them to have pity and to take care of the souls of their relatives, to light them on their journeys, and to guide them to the dwelling place of their ancestors. This idea proves that they believe in the immortality of the soul.

The feast being thus concluded, each takes the bones of his relations; they carry them all in their hands and take them to stony places, hollow, rugged and unfrequented; they leave them there, and that is the end of the ceremony. After that, the dead whose feast they have held are never spoken of again in any way, and they remain in perpetual oblivion.

Apparently, by Hubbard's time the influence of Catholic missionaries and other factors had brought about an evolution in the Feast of the Dead. For the Ottawa it had become an annual event celebrated during the May full moon. Hubbard observed that small poles decorated by flaps of white cloth marked the graves. The ceremony began with all tribal members except the young children blackening their faces with charcoal and engaging in a two-day long period of fasting and intense mourning. Then the Indians washed their faces, dressed in gaudy finery and began feasting and celebrating. They also placed bowls of food at the head of each grave. After several days of merriment the ceremony concluded with a grand game of lacrosse. The concept of the Feast of the Dead would continue to evolve into the 20th century. Some Ottawa families still celebrate a "Ghost Supper" each November 1st, including a place setting for the departed.

As he observed the ceremonies at the mouth of the Grand River, Hubbard learned the particulars of the trial in the sand dunes. While making a visit across the Detroit River to Fort Malden, where the British distributed presents annually, members of a band of Manistee Ottawa had befriended a Canadian Indian and invited him to return to their village. There he fell in love with an Ottawa maiden, married her and settled down as a member of the tribe. He proved himself an able hunter and expert trapper, but, according to custom, he had to deliver all proceeds of the chase to his wife's father until the birth of their first child. Eventually they had numerous children but at the time of the drunken quarrel when he stabbed to death the chief's son, he remained nearly destitute, owning but the clothes he wore and a few traps.

Ottawa law in such cases was similar to that of the Old Testament - "an eye for an eye and a tooth for

A Michigan Indian camp as illustrated in Flavius Littlejohn's 1875 collection of Indian legends.

21

a tooth." To satisfy the murdered man's family he to surrender his own life and if he failed to do so justice could be enacted on one of his brothers-in -law. But Ottawa law also provided for mitigating circumstances - such as his being out of his mind - under the influence of the white man's firewater - at the time of the crime. In those cases if the offended family agreed, he might retain his life and satisfy their honor through the gift of furs or other valuables they deemed suitable.

Following the murder, the Indian escaped with his family to a great marsh at the headwaters of the Muskegon River, a celebrated trapping ground. Having but few traps and little ammunition, he set up an extensive trap run of deadfalls, hoping thereby to secure the furs that could save his life. In his absence the chief held a pow-wow with his sons and, knowing the murderer to be a poor man, determined on his death to revenge their honor. But, thinking the family had fled to Canada beyond their reach, they demanded his brothers-in -law answer for the crime. Accordingly, the youngest, an unmarried brave, sent word to the chief that he would return with his brother-in-law and if he failed he would surrender his own life in his stead.

He knew the approximate whereabouts of the fugitive family and after a long and difficult journey, he located them in a miserable plight, nearly starved. The winter, it seems, had been an extraordinary one, of very deep snow followed by a great flood. As a result the Indian had captured next to nothing in his traps. All he had left was his honor. He promised the messenger that he would report to the Feast of the Dead to accept justice.

On the final morning of the celebration, the hollow thump of his drum and his plaintive death song alerted Hubbard that he had arrived. In company with the other traders and Indians he scrambled atop the nearby sand dunes to witness a "scene indelibly

O-KE-MOS.

The name of Ottawa Chief Okemos is perpetuated on the Michigan map.

stamped on my mind, never to be forgotten."

Having made three feinting thrusts of the gleaming blade, the chief's son tightening his hold on the Indian's shoulder and looked long and deep into the eyes of the man who had murdered his brother with that same knife. Still he saw no emotion, not a sign of fear in the face of death. Suddenly he plunged the knife to the hilt in his breast and quickly pulled it out. A jet of hot blood spurted from the wound and still the brave man uttered not a cry of pain - stood their unmoving - as his life blood pooled on the sand before him. Only the chirping of the birds broke the silence of the scene. To Hubbard it seemed an eternity as the Indian stood there motionless, his blood gushing with every beat of his heart. Then his knees began to quiver, his eyes fluttered and he pitched forward on the sand - stone dead.

His family, who had silently watched the execution, now ran to the body of their father and husband and threw themselves on it, wailing piteously.

Hubbard remembered turning to Deschamps, who too was crying, and saying: "Why did you not save that noble Indian? A few blankets and shirts and a little cloth, would have done it." "Oh, my boy," he replied, "We should have done it. It was wrong and thoughtless of us. What a scene we have witnessed."

For fifteen or twenty minutes the chief and his family sat motionless on their rush mats, watching as the Indian's family clung to the body, sobbing their grief, friendless. Alone in the wilderness with no one to provide for them, they too must soon die.

Then the chief arose and standing over the family huddled on the body, said in a voice trembling with emotion: "Woman stop weeping. Your husband was a brave man, and like a brave, was not afraid to die as the rules of our nation demanded. We adopt you and your children in the place of my son; our

Gurdon Hubbard in later life.

lodges are open to you; live with any of us; we will treat you like our own sons and daughters; you shall have our protection and love."

Some of the assembled Indians called out "Che-qui-ock" (that is right) and the tragedy had played its course. That was the Ottawa way - hard but fair, and with a certain symmetry.

Hubbard would experience many other thrilling adventures over the course of the succeeding decade as he continued to follow the colorful life of the Indian trader. He spent the winter of 1819-1820 trading at the mouth of the Muskegon River and the following winter made his headquarters a post at the future site of Kalamazoo, near the present intersection of Riverview Drive and Gull Road.

Hubbard left the fur trade in 1834, to cast his lot with the frontier settlement of Chicago. He became one of the city's most prominent citizens, earning a fortune in the meat packing industry and shipping enterprises. He lost most of that fortune in the 1860s as a result of fire and shipwrecks. The Chicago Fire of 1871 all but finished him off financially.

Left with little save the "The Lilacs" cottage he had constructed on his beloved Mackinac Island, Hubbard spent the remainder of his days promoting his real estate ventures there. In fair weather he often sat on his cottage porch, gazing out over the Straits of Mackinac, reliving the glorious days of his youth seven decades before when in quest of furs he paddled the length of Lake Michigan 26 times in birch bark bateaux. But of all his many adventures the one he remembered as "the grandest and most thrilling incident of my life" was the execution of the brave Indian at the mouth of the Grand River, Michigan Territory, in 1819.

Greasy, Grimey – But Good:
Voyageur Vittles

Ah, the voyageurs - what men they were. Clad in bright sashes and jaunty plumed hats, those devil-may-care French-Canadians won fame as the workhorses of the upper Great Lakes fur trade. Their steel sinews paddled the big birch bark bateaux carrying the first white men to gaze with awe on the vast inland seas that lap Michigan's shores, the black robbed Jesuit priests who brought the cross to the wilderness and the generations of Indian traders whose lust for fur dominated the economy of the Great Lakes for centuries.

They were the men of which legends are made - short by modern standards - averaging five feet four inches, but with great broad shoulders and barrel chests - capable of almost superhuman feats of strength and endurance. Able to dip their red-painted paddles at the rate of 50 strokes a minute all day long and well into the night if need be - stopping but once each hour for a few puffs of their clay pipes, then back to their task.

The canoe became their home. In it all day, they slept under the craft at night. When they encountered rapids where sharp rocks might pierce its fragile birch bark bottom, they quickly unloaded the cargo - three tons or more of trade goods, furs and supplies - then two men ran with the canoe and the other six to ten voyageurs hefted 90 pound packs to their backs. Aided by a tumpline across their foreheads, they slung two, three, four - celebrated voyageurs carried as many as five bundles at a time - and away they trotted along the portage path.

Despite such rigors, voyageurs retained enough energy to woe many an Ottawa, Chippewa, Potawatomi and Cree maiden. Some boasted a dozen pretty Indian wives!

Canoeing, portaging, wenching, it was all the same to those unlettered sons of the forest - as long as they were moving and were free. Their merry voyageur songs echoed from the Pictured Rocks to the Straits of Detroit:

En roulant ma boule roulant
En roulant ma boule
En roulant ma boule roulant
En roulant ma boule

Needless to say, such Herculean labors inspired an equally epic appetite. The huge quantities of food wolfed down by hungry voyageurs astonished many a visitor to the north country. Thomas Simpson, who utilized Canadian voyageurs in an attempt to reach the Arctic in the 1830s, described a daily ration of twelve pounds of venison or four or five big whitefish allotted to each man. "Yet," he recorded, "there was one of them who complained he had not enough, and did not scruple to help himself to an additional supply whenever the opportunity offered: it would have taken twenty pounds of animal food daily to satisfy him."

But, the traditional boast of the Northwest Fur Company voyageurs that they could "live hard, lie hard, sleep hard and eat dogs!" implies that such ample rations could not always be expected.

Canine cookery aside, the voyageurs developed a distinctive culinary tradition, part French, part Indian, and shaped by the necessities of their fast paced wilderness travel and travail. No dainty dish, this voyageur cuisine, it was hearty, robust, calculated to stick to the ribs of a man ready to eat a dog. And whatever else it lacked by way of seasoning, one ingredient was prerequisite - grease, and plenty of it.

Bear grease, in particular, it seems, was

Voyageurs built up an appetite by paddling from dawn to dusk, shooting rapids and portaging.

considered a delicacy. Robert M. Ballantyne, a young Englishman who spent six months as a clerk with the Hudson's Bay Company in 1841, was traveling from Sault Ste. Marie to Montreal when his voyageurs discovered a great prize while gathering firewood - a big mocock of bear grease that had been cached by some Indians. The Indian's loss was the voyageurs greasy gain and "ere two days were passed the whole of it was eaten by the men, who buttered their flour cakes with it profusely." Lacking bear grease, voyageurs utilized pork grease, venison grease, buffalo grease, racoon grease or goose grease. Frequently it transcended mere grease and became tallow - the stuff of which old-fashioned candles were molded.

Understandably, non-voyageurs found tallow less than pleasing to the palate. Capt. Thomas G. Anderson, a Canadian who spent 58 years as a trader and Indian agent on the upper Great Lakes frontier, graphically described an experience with tallow in 1807:

I would sometimes have venison fried in deer's tallow in the kettle, or in the long frying pan. These steaks I could not eat hot enough to prevent their congealing in their progress to my throat; consequently the roof of my mouth would become so thickly cased over with tallow as to necessitate the use of my knife to remove it.

So important was food in the life of the voyageur that diet formed a basis for class distinction. Novice voyageurs, who could be trusted only with canoeing and carrying and returned to civilization each season, were derisively called *mangeur de lard* (pork-eater) because their ordinary fare consisted of dried peas boiled in pork fat. Actually they received peas only on the voyage from Montreal to Mackinac

Island, the hub of a fur trading empire that stretched for a thousand miles and more to the west and north. At Mackinac Island and during their further travels the daily soups contained pounded, leached Indian corn in lieu of peas.

Gurdon S. Hubbard, a 15-year-old Vermonter who launched his colorful career as a fur trader in 1818, recorded that on Mackinac Island: "The daily ration issued by the commissary to a mess of from six to ten men, consisted of one pint of lyed or hulled and dried corn, with from two to four ounces of tallow, to each man; and this was all the food they received, except that on Saturday flour was given them for Sunday pancakes." Used to the pork, peas and hard bread they had eaten en route to the island, some of the *mangeurs de lard* grew angry and complained. But, as Hubbard observed, the old voyageurs soon quieted them down, telling them "that many of them would be thankful for even that before they returned from their winter quarters.

Despite his troubles with venison tallow Anderson had enjoyed his initial encounter with the pork-eater style of voyageur cookery while traveling to Mackinac Island in 1800:

The men's practice in the culinary art was very simple, but good. The tin kettle, in which they cooked their food, would hold eight or ten gallons. It was hung over the fire, nearly full of water, then nine quarts of peas--one quart per man, the daily allowance--were put in; and when they were well bursted, two or three pounds of pork, cut into strips, for seasoning, were added and all allowed to boil or simmer till daylight, when the cook added four biscuits, broken up, to the mess, and invited all hands to breakfast. The swelling of the peas and biscuit had now filled the kettle to the brim, so thick that a stick would stand upright in it. It looked inviting, and I begged for a plate full of it, and ate little else during the journey. The men now squatted in a circle, the kettle in their midst, and each one plying his wooden spoon or ladle from kettle to mouth, with almost electric speed, soon filled every cavity.

The higher caste of voyageurs, *hivernants* or winterers, seasoned men who plied the distant waters and who spent the winter trading in the wilderness, received special rations of meat, bread and wine when they returned from their far flung trading posts. But en route they relied on pemmican as a staple. Made from pounded and dried buffalo meat or sometimes venison, moose or other game, mixed with ample grease and perhaps seasoned with berries, pemmican kept well and was easily transported.

Egerton Ryerson Young, who launched a lengthy career as missionary to the Canadian Indians in 1868, described the preparation of pemmican:

When the Indian or half-breed hunters succeeded in killing a large number of buffaloes, after being skinned the meat was skillfully cut off in large thin flakes and strips. These were placed on a frame staging. Utilizing the heat and warmth of the sun above, and a small, fire made of buffalo chips below, these thin sheets of meat were soon dry as they could be. The next step in the process was to pound this dry meat as fine and small as possible. Large bags, capable of holding from one to three bushels, were made by the squaws out of the fresh buffalo hides, with the fur side out. Into these green hide-bags this pounded dry meat was packed. To aid in the packing down an Indian in his dirty moccasined feet, would frequently jump into the bag and stamp and dance around in it as it was held up by two other strong, sturdy, fellows,

Voyageurs eagerly awaited the rubbaboo to boil.

while a fourth kept shoveling in additional meat until no more could be packed in. Then the melted buffalo tallow was poured in until it permeated the whole mass. The top of the bag was then skillfully sewed together with sinew, and it was ready for use. If well prepared it would keep for years. This pemmican was the most nourishing food I ever ate, but a little would go a long way, for it often smelled like rotten soap-grease.

Perhaps because of that malodorous quality, if they had time, voyageurs preferred to consume pemmican in a soup called rubbaboo.

Robert Kennicott, a young Chicago scientist who studied the natural history of the Canadian Northwest in the 1850s and 1860s, observed:

Rubbaboo is a favorite dish with the northern voyageurs when they can get it. It consists simply of pemmican made into a kind of soup by boiling in water. Flour is added when it can be obtained, and it is generally considered more palatable with a little sugar. Pemmican is supposed by the benighted world outside to consist only of pounded meat and grease; an egregious error; for, from experience on the subject, I am authorized to state that hair, sticks, spruce leaves, stones, sand etc., enter into its composition, often quite largely.

The journal of the Rev. Peter Jacobs, a Methodist missionary to the northern Indians in the 1850s, offers a detailed description of the preparation of rubbaboo, the most essential part being to keep the flour-soup constantly stirred to prevent it from burning on the bottom of the pot. The Rev. Jacobs also recorded the manner in which voyageurs consumed the delicacy: "Very often the men, when they are in a great hurry, instead of using dishes and spoons, pour out their rubbaboo on the smooth hollow rocks, where it becomes cooler in a short time, and eat it; those who have no spoons generally eat it in the dog fashion, licking it up with their tongues." Such were the sights to be observed in frontier Michigan - gaily dressed French canoeists lapping soup off stones at the water's edge.

Once the hivernants reached their winter headquarters, fish became the staple diet. For that reason, invariably they chose a site that offered good fishing, supplementing what they caught by bagging an occasional deer or other game animal and by wild rice and mococks of maple sugar traded from the Indians. Voyageurs prepared fish in a variety of ways but fish soup was a favorite. James McKenzie, who made a "canoe jaunt" into northern Canada in 1808, long remembered a New Year's feast where a voyageur "with hands which have not seen a drop of water since last New Year's Day, made a large kettle full of boulettes of fish, each as big and ill shaped as his own head."

Fur traders who wintered to the south enjoyed more varied game, depending on the luck of the hunt. During Hubbard's first season of trading in the Illinois country during the winter of 1818-1819, he and his voyageur crew ate venision, raccoon, bear, turkey, swans, geese, ducks and cranes. Voracious eaters that they were, anything that happened there way, even an occasional panther, ended up in their stomachs. Lotus seeds gathered from ponds provided a coffee substitute and the woods abounded with bee trees. They kept a large wooden trough full of honey all through the winter and "partook whenever we desired."

Hubbard's trading party considered them-selves fortunate in possessing an iron bake-pan. This permitted the cooking of whatever game they secured in French style, which Hubbard thought, "could not

Laurence Oliphant, who toured Lake Superior in 1854, sketched this view of a voyageur's camp.

be excelled in any kitchen." Hubbard's autobiography preserves two recipes he enjoyed during that first winter in the Illinois country:

> To one pound of lean venison, add one pound of the breast of turkey, three-fourths of a pound of the fat of bear or raccoon; salt and pepper to taste, and season with the wild onion or leek; chop up or pound fine the meat, and mix all well together; then make a thin crust, with which cover the sides and bottom of the back pan; then put in the meat and cover it with a thicker crust, which must be attached firmly to the side crust; now put on the cover of your bake pan and set it on the hot coals, keeping them on the top, and bake for one hour, and you will have a delicious dish.
> Another: Make a thin batter and drop small balls of the minced meat into it and fry in bear or coon fat, taking care that the meat is well covered with the batter. This we called "les avingnol."

The gourmet delights Hubbard enjoyed during his first season of trading were not necessarily standard fare during other years. He spent the winter of 1826-1827 trading in the Kankakee vincinity. Game was so scarce that his voyageurs survived in a state of semi-starvation, subsisting almost entirely on corn. Then, one spring day Hubbard discovered that the camp mascot, a large domestic tom cat, had gnawed the ends of some of his prize furs, greatly reducing their value. Enraged, he shot the cat and threw it to his Indian cook telling him that the pelt would make him a nice tobacco pouch. But let us allow Hubbard, himself, to tell what befell the feline corpus delicti:

> Just before dinner time I went out again and asked the cook what he had done with the cat. He

answered me by pointing to the kettle in which the corn soup was cooking for the men's dinner. I laughed, but said nothing.

When the men came in and smelled the savory stew they were greatly pleased at the thought of having meat for dinner. They were always in the habit of selecting the choicest bits of meat and sending them to me, and they did not forget me on this occasion; but I declined to eat, telling them I did not care for it, and that they could eat all of it. They ate it with great relish and after they had finished their dinner, I asked them if they knew what they had eaten? They said "yes, wildcat," and they were greatly astonished when I told them they had devoured our old tom cat. One of them said it made no difference, it was good, the other thought differently, and tried hard to rid himself of what he had eaten by thrusting his finger down his throat, but without success; the old cat would not come up

Dr. Chandler Robbins Gilman, employed voyageurs from Mackinac Island for a pleasure trip to the Pictured Rocks in 1835. This first tourist to visit the Lake Superior region recorded a happier experience with a meal prepared by voyageurs at Whitefish Point. One of them:

...mixed flour, water and salt together, into a stiff dough, without either yeast, pearlash, or butter; and formed this into a cake about two inches thick, and of a size and shape to fill the frying pan in which it was to be baked. As, however, the fire was very hot, the bread began to burn below before it was well warmed atop; then it was turned, and thus, by frequent turnings, before the outside was quite as black as my hat, the inside was warmed through; some whitefish, salt pork, and dough balls, had

North country cookery included game on a stake.

been all the while boiling together in our big camp kettle; and by the time he had finished baking three or four cakes, the boiling mess was cooked and poured out into a deep tin pan; pork, fish, dough balls and no inconsiderable portion of the liquor, called by the men soup, all together.

Despite initial misgivings, Gilman sat down to a voyageur feast. He admitted "Really I never enjoyed anything so much in all my life."

While encamped at Whitefish Point waiting for a storm to abate so he could continue on to Sault Ste. Marie, Gilman sampled another specimen of voyageur cookery - roasted smoked trout. A voyageur:

...cut a white cedar stick, about three feet long and an inch in diameter; this he split for two thirds of its length, then placed the fish lengthwise in the fork, and tied the ends together at the top. This, of course, held the fish fast, but did not spread it out. For that purpose he took small thin cedar sticks, four or five inches long, and placed them between the fish and the wood, first on the one side then on the other. Thus it was kept open and fully exposed to the fire near which the stick was now stuck in the ground at the proper angle so as to project sufficiently over the fire to cook, and yet not be exposed to the smoke or in danger of falling. When, after four or five turnings, he pronounced it done, it was very nice eating with plenty of salt.

Voyageurs practiced a similar camp fire cookery using sticks to bake bread. During his first canoe journey to Lake Superior in 1868, Young watched with amusement the less than hygienic culinary art of an Indian voyageur:

Having no baking pan in which to pour out his flour, he proceeded to clear away the dust and leaves from a granite rock that cropped up to the surface nearby. His moccasined foot performed that operation sufficiently to suit his simple taste. Then from the bag he poured out fifteen or twenty pounds of flour on this spot. Having no dish in which to bring water from the river to mix with his flour, he found a capital substitute in his dirty old greasy felt hat. Several trips down to the river gave him sufficient, and soon he had the whole deftly mixed into dough.

His next move was to build up a capital fire, and then, from the willows near the shore, to supply himself with quite a number of sticks about the size and length of ordinary walking canes. Then spitting on his hands he attacked that pile of dough. He tore off a piece weighing about a pound, and after kneading it and rolling it between his hands he stuck the lump on the end of one of those cane like sticks then skillfully working the dough down a little way he flattened it out into the shape of and what is really called, a "beaver's tail." Carefully pushing the other end of the stick down into the soft ground near the fire, the trowel - like cake was slanted to the right distance near the fire to be cooked. When one side was done brown it was turned over, and soon the "beaver tails" were ready for the hungry men.

As they traveled, voyageurs augmented their beaver tail bread, pea soup, corn chowder or rubbaboo with berries, turtles, fish and any other hapless creature including, hawks, crows, seagulls and song birds, they happened to get their hands on.

Those who discovered eggs counted themselves particularly fortunate. Kennicott described the finding of a ruffed grouse nest

While pulling their crafts up rapids voyageurs kept alert for turtle eggs.

containing five eggs. One of the voyageurs used them to make a treat called *gallette*. It was simply prepared, according to Kennicott: "the flour bag is opened and a small hollow made in the flour, into which a little water is poured, and the dough is thus mixed in the bag; nothing is added, except, perhaps some dirt from the cook's unwashed hands, with which he kneads it into flat cakes, which are baked before the fire in a frying pan, or cooked in grease."

Anderson, the old Canadian frontiersman, never forgot the time in 1814 when while to Mackinac Island he allowed his voyageurs to collect turtle eggs on the sandy shores as they pulled the canoe through the rough water:

But the eating of turtle's eggs was, after a few days, brought to a sudden termination. These eggs are somewhat less in size than pigeon's. My cook brought me, as usual, a dozen for breakfast. On opening the first one, I observed something coiled in it, like a black hair; but how a hair could get inside of an egg, I could not make out. So I summoned the men to examine the phenomenon. They at once called out, "a snake." I was not aware till then that turtles' and rattlesnakes' eggs were quite similar, and that they both made their deposits in the sand, for the warmth of the sun to hatch; nor did I know how many young snakes I may have eaten. We had collected of the mixed kinds, and eaten at least a peck a day for the last five days, and I now regretted the discovery, for they were very good. But our stomachs revolted against them for further indulgence.

Col. Thomas McKenney, an Indian agent who traversed lakes Huron and Superior en route to treaty negotiations at Fond du Lac in 1826, noted well the voyageur's "disposition to kill and eat whatever fell their way." A bird lover, McKenney remained alert to protect his avian friends from ending up in the rubbaboo pot. While camped on the Keweenaw Peninsula, he discovered a nest of blue birds in a dead tree. He gave the voyageurs strict orders that the baby birds were not to be molested.

Later, north of the mouth of the Ontonagon River, McKenney spied a bird approaching from across the lake, so weary from its efforts that it could barely fly. The bird landed atop the small sail the voyageurs had hoisted and immediately one raised his paddle and shouted "Food, Food." McKenney grabbed his arm before he could bat the bird to death, the sail was lowered and the tired creature handed to its protector. After feeding it cracker crumbs, McKenney secured the bird in a birch bark mocock. He succeeded in getting the bird back to his home in Washington, D.C., where it became a pet. It learned to come to the name McKenney bestowed on it, "Meme," Chippewa for its species - passenger pigeon. Existing in the billions in flocks so dense they darkened the sky like an eclipse of the sun as late as the 1870s, the last passenger pigeon on earth died in a Cincinnati zoo in 1914.

So also have the colorful breed of men known as voyageurs disappeared. Their vocation has descended to another class of men and women, who steer great roaring vehicles laden with modern society's needs. Truckers too have developed a distinctive culinary tradition - everyone knows "where trucks are found good foods abound."

But few of these diesel powered voyageurs would welcome the ancient fare - steaming ladles of rubbaboo, turtle eggs sunny side up and platters heaped high with beaver tail bread. Fewer still would be so adventurous as to dine in the time honored voyageur way - sans spoon, sans bowl.

Mackinac Memories:
The First Two Centuries

Chippewa chiefs and Ottawa legends, black-robed priests and coureurs de bois, merry voyageur songs and the cannon's boom, palisaded forts and red-coated soldiers, scalping knives and tomahawks, white caps and whitefish, birch bark bateaux, tall masted schooners, whaleback ore boats belching plumes of black smoke, fast ferry rides to a fairy island, fur traders, fishermen, fudge hawkers, two gleaming harps of steel that link Michigan's majestic peninsulas - this is the lore and the lure of the Straits of Mackinac.

To visit Mackinac is to fall under its spell and to never forget. And of the thousands who came during its first two centuries of recorded history many wrote accounts of what they saw and experienced. Those words survive the writers to offer pen pictures into the past - indelible memories of Mackinac.

Before Mackinac or Mackinaw there was Michilimackinac, designating variously the entire straits region, the forts at present day St. Ignace, Mackinaw City and Mackinac Island or simply the island. The commonly accepted derivation of the Algonquian word Michilimackinac - the Great Turtle, in reference to the shape of Mackinac Island, has been frequently disputed. Henry Rowe Schoolcraft, the famous Indian ethnologist who resided on Mackinac Island in the 1830s, first visited there in 1820. He wrote in his travel narrative published the following year:

The ordinary interpretation of great turtle is not widely amiss; but in its true meaning, the term enters more deeply into the Indian mythology then is conjectured. The island was deemed, in a peculiar sense, the residence of spirits during all its earlier ages. Its cliffs, and dense and dark groves of maples, beech, and iron-wood, cast fearful shadows; and it was landed on then in fearfulness, and regarded far and near as the *Sacred Island*. Its apex is, indeed, the true Indian Olympus of the tribes, whose superstition and mythology peopled it by gods, or manitos.

Andrew Blackbird, an educated Ottawa from the Harbor Springs area, gave an entirely different version based on his people's oral traditions in his *History of the Ottawa and Chippewa Indians of Michigan* published in 1887:

Our tradition says that when the Island was first discovered by the Ottawas, which was some time before America was known as an existing country by the white man, there was a small independent tribe, a remnant race of Indians who occupied this island, who became confederated with the Ottawas when the Ottawas were living at Manitoulin, formerly called Ottawa Island, which is situated north of Lake Huron. The Ottawas thought a good deal of this unfortunate race of people, as they were kind of an interesting sort of people; but, unfortunately, they had most powerful enemies, who every now and then would come among them to make war with them. Their enemies were of the Iroquois of New York. Therefore, once in the dead of the winter while the Ottawas were having a great jubilee and war dances at their island, now Manitoulin, on account of the great conquest over the We-ne-be-goes of Wisconsin, during which time the Senecas of New York, of the Iroquois family of Indians, came upon the remnant race and fought them, and almost entirely annihilated them. But two escaped to tell the story, who effected their escape by flight and

46

by hiding in one of the natural caves at the island, and therefore that was the end of this race. And according to our understanding and traditions the tribal name of those disastrous people was "Mi-shi-ne-macki-naw-go," which is still existing to this day as a monument of their former existence; for the Ottawa and Chippewa named this little island "Mi-shi-ne-macki-nong" for memorial sake of those their former confederates, which word is the locative case of the Indian noun "Michinemackinawgo." Therefore, we contend, this is properly where the name Michilimackinac is originated.

The beauty of the Mackinac country remained solely to be appreciated by the native Americans of succeeding cultures until 1634 when Jean Nicolet, a French coureur de bois in quest of the fabled route across the continent to the Orient, became the first known European to pass through its waters. En route to the "people of the sea" who he believed to be Asians, Nicolet held a grand conference at Green Bay among the native Winnebago. Nicolet recorded no account of his explorations but in 1642 Father Barthelemy Vimont first wrote of his friend's exploits. He described Nicolet's arrival at Green Bay:

He wore a grand robe of China damask, all strewn with flowers and birds of many colours. No sooner did they perceive him than the women and children fled, at the sight of a man who carried thunder in both hands - for this they called the two pistols he held. The news of his coming quickly spread to the places round about and there assembled four or five thousand men. Each of the chiefs made a feast for him, and at one of these banquets they served at least six beavers.

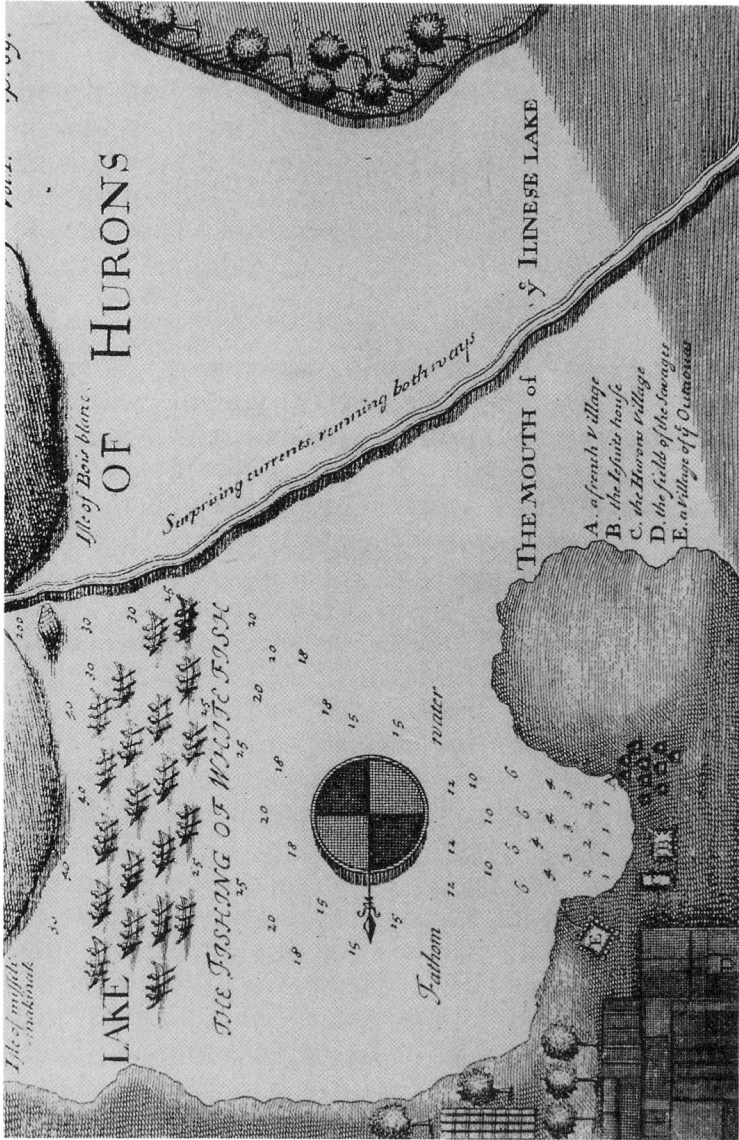

Louis Lahontan's 1688 map of the Straits of Mackinac.

Vimont's description appeared first in the *Jesuit Relations,* yearly reports of missionary activities sent in manuscript to Paris where they were printed in French from 1633-1673. These rich sources contain the first printed information about the Mackinac region, including the exploits of Pierre Esprit, Sieur de Radisson, and Medart Chouart, Sieur de Groseilliers, the next Europeans to pass through the straits, 24 years after Nicolet's feat. In the *Relation* of 1669, Father Jean Claude Allouez recorded the first mention of Mackinac Island. Father Claude Dablon wrote a detailed description of the straits in the *Relation* of 1671. Like my later visitors, he marveled at the size and quantity of the fish caught there:

This spot is the most noted in all these regions for its abundance of fish, since, in savage parlance, this is its native country. No other place, however it may abound in fish is properly its abode, which is only in the neighborhood of Michilimackinac.
In fact, besides the fish common to all the other Nations, as the herring, carp, pike, golden fish, whitefish, and sturgeon, there are here found three kinds of trout; one, the common kind, the second, larger, being three feet in length and one in width; and the third, monstrous, for no other word expresses it, - being moreover so fat that the Savages, who delight in grease, have difficulty in eating it. Now they are so abundant that one man will pierce with his javelin as many as 40 or 50 under the ice in three hours' time.

Dablon had begun an Indian mission on Mackinac Island during the winter of 1670-71. The following summer he instructed Father Jacques Marquette to reestablish the mission on the northern shore of the straits. Marquette designated his mission

St. Ignace, in honor of the founder of the Jesuits. Two years later Marquette and Louis Jolliet paddled away from St. Ignace on an exploratory expedition that would take them down the Mississippi River. Marquette would never again see his beloved Mission St. Ignace. Six years after Marquette's death near Ludington in 1675, his account of those travels was published in Paris. The distinguished Catholic historian, John Gilmary Shea, first made available an English translation in 1852. Marquette described the exhilaration of his departure from St. Ignace on May 17, 1673:

> We were not long in preparing our outfit, although we were embarking on a voyage the duration of which we could not foresee. Indian corn, with some dried meat, was our whole stock of provisions. With this we set out in two bark canoes, M. Jolliet, myself, and five men, firmly resolved to do all and suffer all for so glorious an enterprise... Our joy at being chosen for this expedition roused our courage, and sweetened the labor of rowing from morning till night.

Six years after Marquette had bid farewell to the straits, the *Griffin*, the first sailing vessel to ply the waters of the upper Great Lakes, anchored in East Moran Bay at St. Ignace. Built the previous winter and spring near Buffalo, the *Griffin* carried Robert Cavelier, Sieur de La Salle, and crew on a mission of exploration and fur trading. Laden with furs, the vessel would mysteriously disappear while sailing back from Green Bay to Niagara Falls. Louis Hennepin, a Recollet priest who accompanied the La Salle expedition, published an account of the voyage in 1683. Despite the rascally friar's penchant for exaggeration and falsehood the volume remains one of the few primary sources for this fascinating episode. Hennepin described St. Ignace as containing two large palisided villages occupied by Huron and Ottawa who practiced a bustling fishing industry:

And in this bay where the *Griffin* was riding at anchor, we looked with pleasure at this large well equipped vessel, amid a hundred or a hundred and twenty bark canoes coming and going from taking whitefish, which these Indians catch with nets, which they stretch sometime in fifteen or twenty fathoms of water and without which they could not subside.

In 1688, a 22-year-old soldier, Baron Louis Armond de Lahontan, left his post at Fort St. Joseph on Lake St. Clair to travel to the little French military and trading station that had been established at St. Ignace. There he hoped to obtain corn from the Indians. In his *New Voyages to North America* published in 1703, Lahontan elaborated on whitefish cuisine and Indian fishing techniques:

You can scarce believe; Sir, what vast schools of whitefish are catched about the middle of the channel, between the continent and the isle of Michilimackinac. The Ottawas and the Hurons could never subside here, without that fishery; for they are obliged to travel about twenty leagues in the woods, before they can kill any harts (deer) or elks, and it would be an infinite fatigue to carry their carcasses so far over land. This sort of whitefish in my opinion, is the only one in all these lakes that can be called good; and indeed it goes beyond all other sorts of river fish. Above all, it has one singular property, namely, that all sorts of sauces spoil it, so that 'tis always eat either boiled or broiled, without any manner of seasoning. In the channels I now speak of the currents are so

51

strong, that they sometimes suck in the nets, though they are two or three leagues off... Here the savages catch trouts as big as one's thigh, with a sort of fishing hook made in the form of an awl, and made fast to a piece of brass wire, which is joined to a line that reaches to the bottom of the lake. This sort of fishery is carried on not only with hooks, but with nets, and that in winter, as well as summer: for they make holes in the ice at a certain distance one from another, thro' which they conduct the nets with poles.

In August, 1691, Father Sebastian Rale' left Quebec for a new missionary post among the Illinois Indians. Reaching Michilimackinac too late in the season to attempt the rest of his journey, he spent the winter and spring there with the two resident priests and busied himself collecting lore from the local Ottawa. Shortly after Rale's death at the hands of an English raiding party at Norridgewock, Maine, some of what he had observed at the straits appeared in *Lettres Edifiantes et Curieuses* (Paris, 1726). He described, for an example, an Ottawa tradition that survived into the Twentieth Century:

They call *Michibichi* the manitou of the waters and of the fish, and they make a sacrifice to him nearly similar when they go to fish or when they undertake a journey. This sacrifice consists of throwing into the water some tobacco, food, kettles, and asking him that the waters of the river should flow more slowly, that the rocks should not break their canoes, and that he accord to them fish in abundance.

Two years before Rale's sojourn at St. Ignace, the first of the French and Indian Wars, known as King William's War, broke out. Until the French finally lost their North American empire in the Treaty of Paris of 1763, intermittently these wars would bloody the frontier as the French and their Algonquian allies pitted themselves in ruthless warfare against the British and their Iroquois allies. In 1690, in an effort to secure control of the strategic Straits of Mackinac, Governor of New France Louis de Buade, Compte de Frontenac, dispatched Louis de la Porte, Sieur de Louvigny, with a detachment of troops to St. Ignace. There the French constructed Fort de Buade, named in the governor's honor. The garrison remained of little military value until the arrival in 1694 of a tough new commandant, Antoine de la Mothe Cadillac.

Cadillac penned a fine description of life at the straits, but it remained in manuscript form until its publication in French in a collection of memoirs and documents edited by Pierre Margry in 1883. The first complete English edition of Cadillac's memoirs appeared in the Lakeside Classics volume for 1947 edited by Milo Quaife. Like many later commentators, Cadillac thought highly of the salubrious climate of the straits although he accepted the testimony of the old Indians there with a "grain of salt:"

It is always healthy at Michilimackinac; this may be attributed to the good air or to the good food, but it is better to attribute it to both. A certain proof of the excellence of the climate is to see the old men there, whose grandsons are growing gray, and it would seem as if death had no power to carry off these specters. They have good hearing and good sight, but their memory often plays tricks on them, for they sometimes claim that they are 150 or 200 years old. They tell tales and recount events which they maintain happened at that time, which is not credible; but they have this advantage, that there is no one who can contradict

Henry Rowe Schoolcraft commissioned this drawing of the ruins of Fort Michilimackinac near Mackinaw City as he remembered them in 1820.

54

them or call them liars except by inference.

Despite his testimonial to the healthfulness of life at the straits, in 1701 Cadillac abandoned Fort du Buade, transferring the garrison to the new Fort Pontchartrain he established on the Detroit River. Five years later the Jesuits also gave up their mission at the straits. But the Mackinac country was too strategic to remain abandoned for long. In 1715 Constant Le Marchand de Lignery arrived with a detachment of soldiers. They soon constructed another palisaded fort, this time on the south shore of the straits, near the present site of Mackinaw City.

Father Pierre Francois-Xavier Charlevoix, an erudite Jesuit historian and traveler, arrived at the new Fort Michilimackinac in 1721. He devoted many pages of his travel narrative published in Paris in 1744 to his experiences at Detroit, Mackinac and Fort St. Joseph near present day Niles. He noted that the economy of the post at the straits had not fully recovered from the decline brought about by Cadillac's evacuation:

There is only here a middling village, where there is still a great trade for peltry became it is the passage or the rendezvous of many of the savage nations. The fort is preserved, and the house of the missionaries, who are not much employed at present, having never found much docility among the Ottawas; but the Court thinks their presence necessary, in a place where one must often treat with our allies, to exercise their ministry among the French, who come hither in great numbers. I have been assured that since the settlement of Detroit, and the dispersion of the savages occasioned thereby, many nations of the North who used to bring their peltries hither, have taken the route of Hudson's Bay, by the River Bourbon, and go there to trade with the English.

The great Anglo-French rivalry for a continent's fur trade referred to by Charlevoix would be settled in the British favor with the surrender of Montreal in 1760. In October of that year the French evacuated Fort Michilimackinac. In 1761, English troops under Captain George Etherington re-garrisoned the fort.

The Michigan frontier did not long remain at peace. British arrogance toward the Indians and their tight-fisted trading practices contributed to the outbreak of Pontiac's Conspiracy, "the most formidable Indian resistance that the English speaking people had ever faced." Within weeks after the insurrection erupted in May, 1763, all Great Lakes forts west of Niagara except Detroit had fallen to Pontiac's followers.

On June 2, 1763, Alexander Henry, a young British fur trader, was busy at his desk within Fort Michilimackinac writing letters. Most of the soldiers at the post were intently watching the Chippewa play a game of lacrosse. Suddenly the ball flew over the ramparts of the fort and the contestants raced after it. Hearing a war whoop, Henry glanced out his window to see "a crowd of Indians, within the fort, furiously cutting down and scalping every Englishman they found... and more than one struggling between the knees of an Indian, who, holding him in this manner, scalped him, while yet living."

Henry sought shelter from the massacre by hiding in Mackinac-born French fur trader and fierce border fighter Charles deLanglade's home. Secreting himself in the dark attic, he peered through a hole in the wall to witness "in shapes the foulest and most terrible, the ferocious triumphs of barbarian conquerors. The dead were scalped and mangled; the dying were writhing and shrieking, under the unsatiated knife and tomahawk; and from the bodies of some ripped open, their butchers were drinking the blood, scooped up in the hollow of joined hands, an quaffed amid shouts of rage and victory."

Soon all the British who could be found had been killed. Then Henry heard some Indians enter Langlade's home. As they searched for him he tried to bury himself beneath a heap of birch bark maple sugar buckets. He heard the door to the attic unlock, it burst open and:

> The Indians ascended the stairs before I had completely crept into a small opening, which presented itself, at one end of the heap. An instant after, four Indians entered the room, all armed with tomahawks, and all besmeared with blood, upon every part of their bodies.
> The die appeared to be cast, I could scarcely breathe; but I thought that the throbbing of my heart occasioned a noise loud enough to betray me. The Indians walked in every direction about the garret, and one of them approached me so closely that at a particular moment had he put forth his hand, he must have touched me. Still, I remained undiscovered; a circumstance to which the dark color of my clothes, and the corner in which I was must have contributed. In a word, after taking several turns in the room, during want of light, in a room which had no window, and in which they told M. Langlade how many they had killed, and how many scalps they had taken, they returned downstairs, and I, with sensations not to be expressed, heard the door, which was the barrier between me and my fate, locked for the second time.

Henry would experience several other close calls before he was rescued by his friend, Chief

Wawatam. The chief hid him on Mackinac Island in what would become the tourist attraction known as Skull Cave. Henry recorded his thrilling Mackinac adventures and many others experienced during his 16 years as a fur trader in the classic *Travels and Adventures in Canada...* (New York, 1809). Charles de Langlade would continue to win distinction as "the terror of the frontier" participating in 99 battles and skirmishes during the French and Indian Wars and the Revolutionary War prior to his death in 1800.

In August, 1766, Fort Michilimakinac welcomed its new commandant, Maj. Robert Rogers, an intrepid leader who rivaled Langlade in Indian style frontier fighting. The previous year Rogers had penned a description of the straits in his *Concise Account of North America:*

> At the point adjoining Lake Michigan, and for five or six miles from it, south, the land is sandy. Here stands our fort of Michilimackinac, a good stockade, near twenty feet high. There are, at this place, some French inhabitiants, who come here for the sake of trading with the Indians, and for the trout fishing, which is here very valuable, the trout in these straits being exceedingly plenty, and of an extraordinary size; some have been taken that weighed upwards of fourscore pounds.

Rogers' tour at Michilimackinac would not be a happy one. His plot to establish there an independent northwestern province, free of fur trading regulations by eastern officials, resulted in his imprisonment for treason and transfer in chains to Montreal for trial. Although he won acquittal, he was not restored to his command and his career continued downhill. He died in poverty in London in 1795.

Jonathan Carver, a fellow veteran of the French and Indian War and a member of Roger's Michili-

BIRD'S EYE VIEW OF MACKINAC ISLAND.

Docks.   2 Village.   3 Ft. Mackinac.   4 Ft. Holmes.   5 Skull Cave.   6 Robinson's Folly.
7 Arch Rock.   8 Sugar Loaf.   9 Scott's Cave.   10 British Landing.   11 Battle Field.
12 Lover's Leap   13 Pontiac's Lookout.   14 Devil's Kitchen.

By the mid 1850s Mackinac Island boasted numerous tourist attractions.

59

mackinac staff, had accompanied him there in 1766. Shortly after his arrival, he set out under Roger's orders, on an expedition to the west in search of the mythical water route to the Pacific Ocean. He traveled over 4,000 miles during the succeeding 14 months and visited 14 nations of Indians before returning in failure to the straits. His travel narrative first published in 1778 offers a description of the fort:

> Michilimackinac, from whence I began my travels, is a fort composed of a strong stockade, and is usually defended by a garrison of one hundred men. It contains about thirty houses, one of which belongs to the governor, and another to the missionary. Several traders also dwell within its fortifications, who find it a convenient situation to traffic with the neighboring nations.

One of those traders mentioned by Carver was John Askin. An Irish immigrant who had served in the French and Indian War, Askin settled at Michilimackinac in 1764. During the next 16 years he prospered there, establishing a wholesale trading operation with goods transported on his own ships. His papers covering the years 1747-1820 appeared in two fat volumes in 1928 and 1931. A letter to a Detroit supplier dated April 28, 1778, reveals that at Michilimackinac, far removed from the stirring events of the Revolutionary War, thoughts centered primarily on much needed trading supplies:

> I hope you will at least be able to procure the greater part of the corn and flour I ordered and much of the former hulled, a disappointment in these articles would in part knock up the north trade and I assure you if less than three or four vessel loads of these things arrive this season, some persons in that back country will perish and the

trade be hurt...

Isolated as Michilimackinac was from the martial glories and birth of a nation taking place in the east, life there was not without its diversions. John Long, a footloose British fur trader who spent the winter of 1779-1780 with a local Chippewa family, recorded an amusing north country version of the Trojan horse in his *Voyages and Travels* published in 1791. A standing order that no Indian women be allowed to sleep within the fort overnight had been in effect since the massacre of 1763. Long, at the urging of some friends in the garrison, attempted to get around that order through a ruse:

> I applied to two soldiers, and asked them if they could spare time to roll a large hogshead of bottled porter from Chippeway Point to the Fort; they told me whenever it suited me they would be ready to assist. Having purchased the hogshead, and got it rolled down the hill whilst the officers were at dinner, I told the squaws of my plan, and having knocked out the head and bung, and bored several holes to admit as much air as possible, desired them to get in, which with some difficulty I persuaded them to do. I then replaced the head, and ran immediately to the soldiers to acquaint them that the porter was ready, and desired their assistance without delay, as I was afraid some of the bottles were broken and it would be proper to examine them as soon as possible.
> The soldiers immediately returned with me, and applying their shoulders to the cask, rolled it up the hill with great labour and fatigue, continually observing that it was very heavy. Just as they arrived at the gate, the commanding officer and the commissary were coming through, and seeing the hogshead, asked the soldiers what they had got

there? They replied it was bottled porter for a trader, who had desired them to roll it from the Point. As a vessel had just then arrived from Detroit, the commanding officer was so satisfied with the account the soldiers gave, that he observed it was very fortunate, for they now should have plenty of good beer to drink. The soldiers had scarcely rolled another turn, when unluckily one of them kicked his foot against a stone, who with the extreme pain he suffered, fell down. The other, not being able to sustain the whole weight, let go his hold, and the hogshead rolled down the hill with great velocity. Just as it came to the bottom the head fell out, and the squaws exhibited the deception. Unfortunately the commanding officer was near at hand when the accident happened, and though it was a manifest breach of his orders, he could not help smiling at the conceit; and looking at the imprisoned females, said to them, "pretty bottled porter indeed!" The squaws were so confused that they ran with the utmost precipitation into the woods, and did not make their appearance for several days.

The year following Long's shenanigans saw the reestablishment of the fort on the more easily defensible heights of Mackinac Island. By the summer of 1781 the garrison had deserted the old fort, transported government property to the island and moved into its new quarters. Unfortunately for the British, the provisions of the Treaty of Paris of 1783 awarded the island and the new fort to the Americans. Not until 1796, however, would the British relinquish the forts at Detroit and Mackinac Island. Four years later, Secretary of War Samuel Dexter sent Uriah Tracy to inspect the northern forts. His report documents the appearance of the fort at that time:

Fort Michilimackinac is an irregular work partly built with a strong wall and partly with pickets; and the parade ground within it is from 100 to 125 feet above the surface of the water. It contains a well of never failing water, a bomb proof used as a magazine, one stone barracks for the use of officers, equal if not superior to any building of the kind in the United States, a good guard house and barracks for soldiers and convenient block houses. This post is strong both by nature and by art and the possession of it has a great influence with the Indians in favor of the United States... On the bank of the strait adjacent to the fort stands a large house which was by the English called Government House and was kept by the British commander of the fort which now belongs to the United States. The island and the country about it is remarkably healthy and very fertile for so high a northern latitude.

In 1807, a distinguished Canadian traveler, Deputy Post Master General George Heriot, paid a visit to Mackinac Island. His description of the fort provides additional detail as to its appearance:

The fort occupies the highest ground; and consists of four wooden block houses forming the angles, the spaces between them being filled with cedar pickets. On the shore below the fort, there are several storehouses and dwellings.

Heriot also recorded a novel explanation for the meaning of the "little barren island's" name. The Indians, he wrote:

Say that Michapous, the chief of the spirits, sojourned long in that vicinity. They believed that a

BOIS BLANC ISLAND.

ROUND ISLAND.

A late 19th Century view of an observation tower that once stood on the site of Fort Holmes.

64

mountain on the border of the lake was the place of his abode: and they called it by his name. It is here, say they, that he first instructed man to fabricate nets for taking fish, and where he has collected the greatest quantity of these finny inhabitants of the waters. On the island he left spirits, named Imackinkos and from these aerial possessors, it has received the appellation of Michilimackinac.

In the summer of 1812 the garrison at Fort Mackinac consisted of 61 men under command of Lt. Porter Hanks. On June 18 the U.S. congress declared war on Great Britain. Nearly a month later word of that event had yet to reach the island. The night of July 16-17 a large force of British soldiers and Indian allies sailed from their fort on St. Joseph Island and landed at a point now known as British Landing. The invaders quickly advanced to the heights at the center of the island overlooking the fort and planted cannons. Faced with overwhelming odds, Hanks surrendered the fort without firing a shot the next morning.

By the summer of 1814 the British had strengthened the walls of what they now called Fort Mackinaw and constructed a blockhouse on the hill to the rear of the fort. On August 4, an American force under Lt. Col. George Croghan landed to the rear of the fort. The British were waiting and soon routed the Americans with artillery fire. Maj. Andrew Hunter Holmes and several other officers died in the attack. Later the Americans renamed the blockhouse the British had built Fort Holmes in his honor.

But American treaty negotiators succeeded where rifles and bayonets had failed. The provisions of the Treaty of Ghent that ended the war on December 25, 1814, restored Mackinac Island to the Americans. On July 18, 1815, the stars and strips again flapped over Fort Mackinac. The British sullenly withdrew to their new fort on Drummond Island. Seven years later the British also lost that island to the Americans and in 1828 the garrison again moved to St. Joseph Island.

The British loss of Drummond Island came as a result of a decision by the joint commission to establish the border between the U.S. and Canada. It began its work in 1817. Maj. Joseph Delafield, who started as a secretary but eventually headed up the American team, left a diary detailing the commission's activities from 1817-1823. It was published in 1943 as *The Unfortified Boundary.* On July 31, 1820, Delafield first laid eyes on Mackinac Island. The following morning he breakfasted with Ramsay Crooks, one of the resident managers of John Jacob Astor's American Fur Company, "at his long table with about thirty fur traders, hardy respectable looking men, mostly Canadians."

Following the War of 1812, Astor had moved quickly to force out competition, thereby gaining a virtual monopoly of the northern fur trade. Mackinac Island became the hub of a far flung trading empire, the annual rendezvous of thousands of voyageurs and fur traders as well as the Indians who arrived each spring for their annual treaty payments. Delafield wrote in his diary "Mackinac owes all its consequences to the fur trade. In the spring it is a bustling little place and more than a thousand people collect here. They disappear again and in winter it is nearly deserted."

Like Delafield, a man destined to make his mark on the north country first saw Mackinac Island the summer of 1820. Henry Rowe Schoolcraft had been appointed geologist on the expedition to the source of the Mississippi River headed by Michigan Territorial Governor Lewis Cass. The expedition left Detroit in three great north country canoes on May

24, 1820. The explorers arrived on Mackinac Island fourteen days later, amid a cannon salute from the fort. Schoolcraft recorded his initial impression of the island in his travel narrative published in 1821:

> Nothing can present a more picturesque or refreshing spectacle to the traveler, wearied with the lifeless monotony of a canoe voyage through Lake Huron, than the first sight of the island of Michilimackinac, which rises from the watery horizon in lofty bluffs imprinting a rugged outline along the sky, and capped with two fortresses on which the American standard is seen conspicuously displayed. A compact town stretches along the narrow plain below the hills, and a beautiful harbor checkered with American vessels at anchor, and Indian canoes rapidly shooting across the water in every direction.

Sometimes, the passengers who traveled in the Indian canoes Schoolcraft saw scurrying across the straits experienced an adventure they never forgot. John J. Bigsby, a member of the British delegation mapping the border with Delafield, stopped off at Mackinac Island in 1823. From there, he hitched a ride to Drummond Island with a party of Ottawa from L'Arbre Croche. The Indians had already collected their annual payments from the Americans and intended to do the same thing from the British. Armed with a ham, a loaf of bread and a bottle of whiskey, Bigsby set out on his foray:

> Running down to the beach with my knapsack and provision bag, I found a little fleet of twenty-five canoes on the point of starting; and was bidden by signs to jump into the canoe nearest me, but seeing no room, I hesitated.
> The craft was not large. On the prow, where there

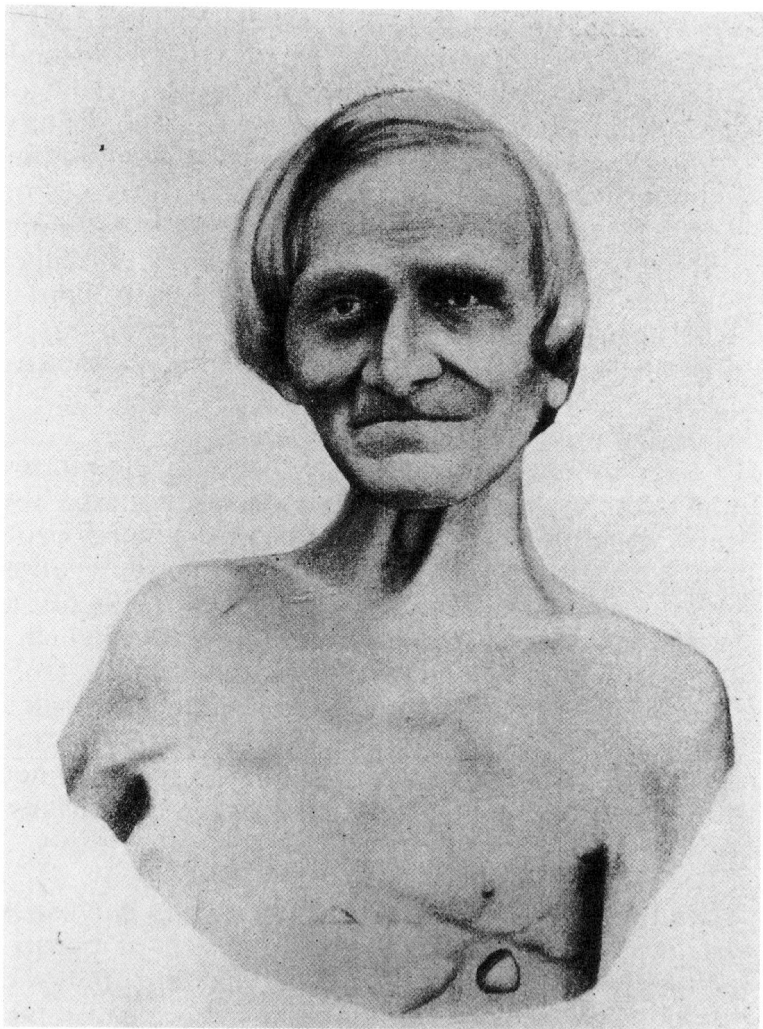

Alexis St. Martin, the "man with the window in his stomach," lived to be 77-years-old and fathered 19 offspring.

was a little shelf, there sat an unquiet little bear, tied with a cord, two smoking Indians and three children sitting on the canoe bottom next to him. Then came four women rowers, among whom I was to squat, or nowhere. The stern half of the canoe was occupied by the Blackbird and a friend, with three more young imps and a steersman. Two or three dogs kept constantly circulating among our legs in search of dropped eatables, who so approved of my ham that I was fain to keep it on my knees.

But we all settled down into a sort of stiff comfort. The water was smooth as glass. The strong unclouded sun was in mid-heavens. We moved away with many an uncouth antic and shriek, both on land and lake.

Two years previous to his visit to Mackinac Island, Bigsby had traveled from Buffalo to Detroit by steamer. Among his fellow passengers was Dr. William Beaumont, enroute back to Fort Mackinac after having been married in Plattsburgh, New York. Beaumont, the post surgeon, would during the summer of 1822 participate in one of the island's most colorful sagas and one which would made medical history. On June 6th, Alexis St. Martin would be accidently shotgunned at point blank range. Gurdon Hubbard, a young American Fur Company trader clerking in the store at the time, witnessed the accident and later recorded it in his autobiography:

This St. Martin was at the time one of the American Fur Company's engages, who, with quite a number of others, was in the store. One of the party was holding a shotgun, which was accidently discharged, the whole charge entering St. Martin's body. The muzzle was not over three feet from him - I think not over two. The wadding entered, as well as pieces of his clothing; his shirt took fire; he fell, as we supposed, dead.

Dr. Beaumont, the surgeon of the fort, was immediately sent for, and reached the wounded man within a very short time - probably three minutes. We had just got him on a cot and were taking off some of his clothing.

After Dr. Beaumont had extracted part of the shot, pieces of clothing, and dressed his wound carefully - Robert Stuart and others assisting - he left him, remarking, "The man can't live thirty-six hours; I will come and see him bye and bye.

But due to Beaumont's medical skill and the 19-year-old voyageur's vigorous constitution he survived. Beaumont's subsequent experiments on St Martin's digestive system would immortalize his patient as "the man with the window in his stomach."

The Robert Stuart, who, according to Hubbard, assisted Beaumont in dressing St. Martin's wound, was at that time the American Fur Company's general manager for the Great Lakes and upper Mississippi River. On October 17, 1822, he wrote his employer, Astor, in New York, a letter concerning his proposed visit to the island. He took the liberty of venturing his opinion on the attractions of life in the straits as opposed to New York:

...This place is more healthy and much more congenial to my means of living, and bringing up my family, for with my present earnings, I could hardly (in New York) rent a house, educate my children, hire a servant, and purchase fuel; and that would never answer, as we are all very fond of eating, and now and then, like a <u>little</u> good drink. And another very substantial blessing is, that we are in a certain degree, removed from the wiles and rougries of the more accomplished part of

A fanciful 19th Century engraving of Arched Rock.

mankind; for here we generally have, at worst, to contend but with small rogues.

The summer of 1826 saw the arrival at Mackinac Island of another party of distinguished visitors. The nation's superintendent of Indian affairs, Thomas L. McKenney, Gov. Cass, Col. George Croghan and other officials were returning from a canoe journey to Fond du Lac, Wisconsin, where they had negotiated an Indian treaty. Landing on the island on August 27, McKenney spent the following three days rambling about. He enjoyed the Arched Rock, Sugar Loaf and the other standard attractions. The island impressed him. What he wrote in his travel narrative published in 1827 rivaled the promotional literature later generated by professional "ad-men."

Mackinac is really worth seeing. I think it by no means improbable, specially should the steamboats extend their route to it, that it will become a place of fashionable resort for the summer. There is no finer summer climate in the world. The purest, sweetest air - lake scenery in all its aged and grand magnificence, and the purest water; white fish in perfection, the very best fish, I believe, in the world, and trout, weighing from five to fifty pounds. No flies, and no mosquitoes, nothing to annoy, but every variety for the eye, the taste, and the imagination, with all that the earth, and water, and sky can furnish, (except good fresh meat, and where such fish are plenty, this can be dispensed with) to make it agreeable and delightful. There are no bilious fevers here; and temperate people may, with something like certainty, if not organically diseased, spin out life's thread to its utmost tenuity. But in winter I would prefer not to be here; and that would form an exception, as to temperature, of at least seven months out of twelve.

McKenney's prophecy came true, but not for a few more years. As late as 1830 only one steam packet a month, during the all-to-short shipping season, made the rounds of the upper lake posts. For most European and American excursionists, a visit to Niagara Falls marked the limits of their western sightseeing. Yet a few bold recreationists did attempt tours to the north country. The Rev. Calvin Colton, a journalist, politician, and Indian rights advocate, traveled to Green Bay in the summer of 1830 to witness an Indian council. Enroute he stopped off at Mackinac Island where he also visited the Sugar Loaf and Arched Rock. The latter, in particular, moved the minister to a heavenly comparision:

> From the giddy summit above, the spectator looks down upon the lake beneath the arch, which has the appearance of an immense gateway erected from the delineations of art. Or, from the bosom of the waters below, he looks up, as to the gate of heaven, inviting him to the celestrial regions.

Not all early visitors to Mackinac Island proved welcome. Some brought death in their wake. In the spring of 1832, the depredations of Black Hawk and his Sauk warriors on the Illinois frontier spread terror across Michigan Territory. Settlers in southern Michigan were certain they would be attacked as the Indians moved toward Detroit. Mackinac Island residents shared that concern. Eliza Chapel, a devoutly religious 24-year-old maiden who had been hired by Robert Stuart to teach his many children, confided to her diary:

> July 4th. No public celebration today, not even the firing of cannon. The commanding officer is

daily expecting orders to leave for Chicago, to aid the troops in this Indian warfare which is daily becoming more alarming. Many among us begin to tremble in fear of their approach to attack Mackinac.

July 7th. Mackinac is now greatly perplexed. Fear and alarm take hold of many. The cause is not the movements of the Indians. We have not had any serious, perhaps I may say any fears from them. God appears to be dealing in judgement with our troops who are ordered to attack them. Three steamboats filled with troops are now on passage. On Saturday the steamer *Thompson* reached our island with three companies of Virginia troops, who had in fifteen days traveled fifteen hundred miles - a wild goose chase we think it. They spent one night in our harbor and left behind them two sick soldiers, whose disease has proved to be the dreaded scourge cholera. The men have both died and others are ill. The two other boats have not arrived and the fears of all are excited lest pestilence is the cause of the delay. Our schools are all closed and fear takes hold in many.

Eleven days later the *Thompson* returned from Chicago and Chapel learned of the horrors of the voyage. Fifty-one soldiers died during the three day passage. When the expedition reached Chicago, it was forced to convert the entire fort into a hospital. Scores more died in Detroit from cholera. At least six Mackinac Island residents succumbed to the disease and the usual hordes of traders cut short their stay on the island for fear of contracting it. The cholera proved a far worse threat than Black Hawk. His braves were annihilated by a force of Illinois militia and regular soldiers on August 2, 1830.

The threat of Indian massacre over and the cholera having run its course, life on the island

Tourists could buy souvenirs from Indians on the beach at
Mackinac Island in 1875.

returned to its normal flow. With the advent of additional steamboats and a fleet of sailing vessels to the north country more travelers stopped off at Mackinac. A pair of refined New Yorkers, Dr. Chandler Robbins Gilman and Maj. Murray Hoffman, became the first to visit Lake Superior purely as tourists in the summer of 1835. Leaving Detroit on the schooner *White Pigeon*, five days of sailing in rough weather brought them to Mackinac Island. They tarried several days before hiring local voyageurs to paddle them to the Pictured Rocks. Gilman found the village on Mackinac in "a very dilapidated condition, fast going to decay." In fact, the island's economy had suffered a serious setback when the American Fur Company moved its headquarters to LaPointe, Wisconsin. No longer would the island ring with the shouts and songs of thousands of gaily dressed voyageurs making their rendezvous.

The economy would recover as the century wore on when the islanders learned to cater to tourists like Gilman. But until then they owed their livelihood to the fort and fishing. And what fishing there was! While sightseeing among the Indian wigwams pitched along the shore, Gilman saw a fishing boat land:

All the idlers along the shore, we among the rest, ran down to the water's edge to see what luck the fishermen had had. Their draught had been very good; with two nets they had taken half a dozen large trout and near a hundred whitefish. One of the trout was so large we were induced to have him weighed; he weighed forty-seven pounds. As some one opened his huge mouth, I saw in his throat the tail of a whitefish. I pointed it out to the Indians, or rather half-breeds, for such the fishermen were, and immediately one of them went to work to pull it out. He tugged a long time in vain, and was at last obliged to cut the mouth a good deal before he could get it. Out it came at last, a whitefish of twenty inches long. I was amused to see the coolness with which the half-breed threw this fish among the others.

That same summer of 1835, George W. Featherstonhaugh, an English geologist on a mineral reconnaisance of the upper Great Lakes, also sailed from Detroit to Mackinac Island by schooner. Following the usual sight-seeing, including Skull Cave and an obligatory visit with Henry Schoolcraft, Featherstonhaugh took a boat ride around the island with an army officer stationed there. They anchored at nearby Round Island "to examine an ancient Indian burial ground." Perhaps his visit to Skull Cave gave him the idea, but in any event, he took the liberty of digging up some graves, carrying away skulls and artifacts as souvenirs. The last laugh was on the pot-hunter, however, for when Featherstonhaugh returned to his room with the booty he discovered the burial site was not as ancient as he thought. He received a well-earned revenge from the grave when he:

...found my hands and my clothes so infected with charnel-house nastiness, that I could not endure myself; so, throwing off all my clothes, and sending them immediately to be washed, I spent more than half an hour scrubbing my hands in vain to purify them: the horrid stench was in my nostrils all the evening; everything smelt of a dissection room; and I must say that I was never wore uncomfortable in my life... On awakening in the morning the first thing I was conscious of was the infernal smell of my disgusting plunder; so I jumped out of bed and armed with brushes and soap, and a bottle of eau de cologne, went to the lake, where I exercised myself most vigorously for half an hour...

after which, I determined to give myself an airing on the summit of the island.

A sour Scottish lawyer, James Logan, made a pleasure trip through the western states and Canada in 1836. Logan paid $8 for passage, including meals, on a schooner from Detroit to Mackinac Island. The vessel left Detroit on September 1, reaching the island eight days later. Despite the lateness of the tourist season Logan found every hotel and boarding house on the island full. Finally he was able to secure the use of a hotel sofa with a cloak for a covering. He woke the next morning to watch in awe as the other hotel guests made a mad dash for breakfast:

> As usual in the States, there was a great rush to breakfast, each individual striving to be before his neighbor. This was occasioned by there being a larger company than the table could admit at once. It reminded me of the theatre, at which, when a star is to shine, a crowd generally assembles half an hour before the doors are opened, and when at length a passage is afforded, the people rush in like a river carrying everything before it. It appears to be a custom in the State of Michigan for every person whether engaged in business or not, to hurry forward to a meal, swallow it as fast as he can,and the moment he is satisfied, leave the table. As one goes out another goes in.

To take advantage of the burgeoning tourist trade, the island clearly needed more hotels and restaurants. But still the curious came, including a growing number of ladies. Harriet Martineau, a distinguished British writer armed with a huge ear trumpet, arrived at the island on July 5, 1836. She had steamed up from Chicago on the *Milwaukee*, en route to Detroit. Determined to stay on schedule, the

The Rev. William Ferry preached at The Old Mission Chuurch, built in 1829.

captain only allowed his passengers a few hours to explore the island while he took on supplies. But due to the assistance of the fort commander, Martineau was able to pack a lot into her short stay. The officer told her that the island was so healthy that "people who want to die must go somewhere else." But when she asked about the climate, he answered, "we have nine months winter, and three months cold weather." The highlight of her sight-seeing was the view from Fort Holmes. She wrote in rapture:

> I can compare it to nothing but to what Noah might have seen, the first bright morning after the deluge. Such a cluster of little paradises rising out of such a congregation of waters, I can hardly fancy to have been seen elsewhere . The capacity of the human eye seems here suddenly enlarged, as if it could see to the verge of the watery creation. Blue, level waters appear to expand for thousands of miles in every direction; wholly unlike any aspect of the sea. Cloud shadows and specks of white vessels, at rare intervals, alone diversify it. Bowery islands rise out of it; bowery promontories stretch down into it; while at one's feet lies the melting beauty which one almost fears will vanish in its softness before one's eyes; the beauty of the shadowy dells and sunny mounds, with browsing cattle, and springing fruit and flowers. Thus, and no otherwise, would I fain think did the world emerge from the flood.

Another cultivated British literary lady, Anna Jameson, sojourned on Mackinac Island in July, 1837. Embarking on a tour of the north country, in part to escape for a while her unhappy marriage to a cold-hearted Toronto judge, Jameson left Detroit on the steamer *Thomas Jefferson*. She enjoyed a pleasant two day's voyage to the island, but she found the only full-fledged hotel there completely full. Fortunately, she was able to secure lodging with the Henry Rowe Schoolcraft family. She soon forged a warm friendship with Jane, Schoolcraft's half-Chippewa wife, and later accompanied her on a canoe trip to visit her Indian relatives in Sault Ste. Marie. Jameson found the Indians encamped on the Mackinac Island beach of special interest. Her travel narrative of this northern tour published in 1838 preserves a skillfully crafted word picture of the Indian camp:

There were more than one hundred wigwams, and round each of these lurked several ill-looking, half-starved, yelping dogs. The women were busied about their children, or making fires and cooking, or pounding Indian corn in a primitive sort of mortar, formed of part of a tree hollowed out, with a heavy rude pestle which they moved up and down as if churning. The dress of the men was very various - the cotton shirt, blue or scarlet leggings, and deer skin moccasins and blanket coat; were most general; but many had no shirt nor vest, merely the cloth leggings, and a blanket thrown round them as drapery; the faces of several being most grotesquely painted. The dress of the women was more uniform,; a cotton shirt, and cloth leggings and moccasins, and a dark blue blanket. Necklaces, silver armlets, silver earrings, and circular, plates of silver fastened on the breast, were the usual ornaments of both sexes. There may be a general equality of rank among the Indians; but there is evidently all that inequality of conditions which difference of character and intellect might naturally produce; there were rich wigwams and poor wigwams; whole families ragged, meagre, and squalid, and others gay with dress and ornaments, fat and well-favored.

Jameson included in her book several Chippewa legends collected by the Schoolcrafts. Indian Agent Schoolcraft also told her a good story:

A distinguished Potawatomi warrior presented himself to the Indian agent at Chicago, and observing that he was a very good man, very good indeed - and a good friend to the Long-knives (the Americans), requested a dram of whiskey. The agent replied, that he never gave whiskey to <u>good</u> men - <u>good</u> men never asked for whiskey and never drank it. It was only <u>bad</u> Indians who asked for whiskey, or liked to drink it. '"Then," replied the Indian quickly in his broken English, "me damn rascal!"

Several other American literary ladies including, Juliette Kinzie, Eliza R. Steele and Sarah M. Fuller, penned vibrant accounts of visits to Mackinac Island during the incipient tourist era. But, feminine travelers were the exception to the rule. Most members of the literati to tour the north country were men.

The summer of 1837, brought the arrival of Capt. Frederick Marryat, British author of popular sea and adventure novels. He thought Martineau, whose book had recently appeared, had not overestimated the appeal of the island. He wrote that it had "the appearance of a fairy isle floating on the water, which is so pure and transparent that you may see down to almost any depth: and the air above is as pure as the water, so that you feel invigorated as you breathe it."

The American flag that flapped over the ramparts of Fort Mackinac during Jameson's and Marryat's visits during the summer of 1837 sported a new star. On January 26, 1837, Michigan had officially joined the Union as the 26th state. Its transition from territory to state had been a difficult

This view of Mackinac Island from the bluff was sketched in 1842.

one owing to a border ruckus with Ohio, known as the Toledo War. The compromise that defused the hostilities awarded the coveted "Toledo Strip" to Ohio and Michigan got the western two-thirds of the Upper Peninsula. Many Michiganders branded that a bad bargain. They changed their minds when Douglass Houghton's geological explorations revealed the region's mineral wealth.

En route to the Keweenaw Peninsula, Houghton's expediton stopped off at Mackinac Island in late May, 1840. At least two members of his team penned impressions of the isiand. Houghton's assistant, Bela Hubbard, later wrote that "no place in the North-west possesses greater historic and traditionary interests." He was enthralled with "the natural beauties and wildness of the island, its situation, enthroned at the apex of the peninsula of Michigan and embracing magnificent views of water and island, its lake breezes and pure cold air, and the excellence of its whitefish..."

Charles W. Penny, a Detroit merchant accompanying the expedition, was not as impressed. One Sunday, after scrambling across Arched Rock, attending the Presbyterian church service and spending the rest of the day conversing, reading and lounging, he complained "they have very long days in Mackinac." He complimented the food he received at his boarding house but then quipped "I have already eaten so many whitefish, that my tail wiggles as I go along the street."

Even Mackinac Island's charms, it seems, could not satisfy everyone. Few were less pleased by their Mackinac Island sightseeing than the occasional brothers of the cloth who landed there. The Rev. John H. Pitezel, a pious Methodist missionary enroute to the Upper Peninsula, where he would spend the following nine years proselytizing the Chippewa, stopped off at the island in 1843. He was thoroughly shocked by what he observed during a walk along the beach through the Indian encampment:

> I saw scenes of woe and wretchedness. Some of the worse than heathen whites, French and half-breeds, had been furnishing the Indians with whiskey, and cheating them out of their money. The direst effects of drunkeness were witnessed among them. Some were raving and fighting, some singing, some dancing, or running and whooping, while in some of the lodges were men, women, and children, rolling and tossing, and making hideous noises or doleful moanings. What a very pandemonium was here seen - all the work of whiskey! My soul sickened at this sight of woe.

Another clergyman, the Rev. James Beaven, an Anglican from Toronto traveling to the Canadian Sault to visit the Rev. William McMurray, Henry Schoolcraft's brother-in-law, spent some time on Mackinac Island in August 1845. He too was grieved by what he witnessed among the wigwams. He wrote: "It is only necessary to go amongst the Indians, and witness their habits, to dissipate the romance which one might feel regarding them." Beaven had a better time commuting with nature by himself and gathering nuts and berries.

No less than three literary travelers stopped at Mackinac Island during the summer of 1846. On a tour of the Great Lakes to sketch Indians, Canadian artist Paul Kane found 2,600 Chippewa and Ottawa camped on Mackinac Island to collect their annual treaty payments, He immediately pitched his own tent among the wigwams and set to work sketching the Indians. He did not stay long however:

> I soon had to remove my tent, from the circum-stances that their famishing dogs, which they keep

for the purpose of hunting and drawing their sleds in winter, contrived to carry off all my provisions, and seemed likely to serve me in the same way. This will appear by no means improbable, when I state that, while I was one evening finishing a sketch, sitting on the ground alone in my tent, with my candle stuck in the earth at my side, one of those audacious brutes unceremoniously dashed in through the entrance, seized the burning candle in his jaws and bolted off with it, leaving me in total darkness.

Monroe-born Charles Lanman, Michigan's first native author of distinction, collected some fascinating Indian legends during his stay on the island in 1846. While he sat on the brow of Arched Rock an Ottawa told him the tradition of the creation of that natural wonder:

Very many winters ago, the sun was regularly in the habit of performing his daily circuit across the heavens, and when the stars made their appearance in the sky, he invariably descended into an immense hole supposed to be located in the remote west. But in the process of time it so happened that a chief of the Ottawas committed an unheard of crime against the person of his own daughter, and the Master of Life became so offended, that he caused a mighty wind to come upon the earth, whereby the rocky hills were made to temble, and the waters which surrounded them to roar with a dreadful noise. During this state of things, which lasted for one whole day, the sun shot through the heavens with an unsteady motion, and when it had reached the zenith suddenly became fixed, as if astonished at the red man's wickedness. All the people of the Ottawa nation were greatly alarmed at this phenomenon, and while they were gazing

Mackinac Island tourists "on a lark" in the 1880s.

upon the luminary, it gradually changed into the color of blood, and with a dreadful noise, as if in a passion, it felt upon the earth. It struck the northern shore of Mackinac, formed the cavity of the Arched Rock, and so entered the earth, from which it issued in the far west, at an early hour on the following morning, and then resumed its usual journey across the heavens.

Nature-loving poet William Cullen Bryant arrived on the steamer *St. Louis* in August, 1846, and spent two days roaming the island. He thought: "the world has not many islands so beautiful as Mackinac." He wrote with regret of "the time, which I suppose is near at hand, when its wild and lonely woods will be intersected with highways, and filled with cottages and boarding houses."

The following summer, Albany, New York, newspaper editor and politician Thurlow Weed took passage at Buffalo on the steamer *Empire* for a trip to Chicago to attend a River and Harbor Improvement Conference. On the return voyage he and other delegates spent a day on Mackinac Island. They enjoyed a frolic typical of that then available for well-to-do visitors. The ship's stewart, named Bloomer, organized the outing:

> The picnic realized all the enjoyment that was anticipated. A delightful spot, with a natural bower, had been selected. Mr. Bloomer had taken care to provide a dainty repast, having with him, also, the cook, waiters, etc.
> After visiting the Sugar Loaf, Arch'd Rock, and other points of interest, the band being in attendance, dancing upon the green commenced. Other rural exercises and sports were resorted to, and kept up with spirit, until dinner was announced. The chowder, as one or two Bos-

tonians affirm, was one over which Mr. Daniel Webster, without loss of culinary character, might have presided. After dinner, the sports of the day were concluded by a grand "steeple chase," in which ladies and gentlemen participated. The ground selected for the chase, though apparently on an even surface, proved to be undulating! The consequence was that several gentlemen who left the starting post with *spirit* and confidence, were either down, or distanced by the ladies. One gentleman attributed his fall to the circumstance that Mr. Bloomer, in compounding his "lemonade," had substituted champagne for water.

A more dignified party of travelers arrived at Mackinac Island the summer of 1848, when 16 professors and students from eastern colleges, members of a scientific expedition to Lake Superior headed by naturalist Louis Agassiz, stopped over for a day. J. Elliot Cabot of Boston wrote a narrative of the trip. Apparently, by that year the islanders had begun to appreciate the potential of the tourist industry:

We landed on the little wooden wharf in face of a row of shabby stores, with "Indian Curiosities"posted up in large letters to attract the steamboat passengers during the brief stop for fish. Over their roofs appeared the whitewashed buildings of the fort stretching along the ridge. The inhabitants of the place, looking down upon us from all sides, as from the lower benches of a theatre, soon perceived that we had not departed with the steamer, and we were soon plied with invitations to the two principal lodging houses.

Each year witnessed more of the islanders' energies devoted to harvesting tourist dollars during the all-too-short summer season. And each summer, it seemed, more tourists discovered the island's attractions. Those with literary leanings often wrote about their experiences. The ensueing plethera of travel narratives, guide books, promotional pamphlets, magazines and newspaper articles further advertised the charm of the straits.

James Jesse Strang, the charismatic "king of Beaver Island," wrote and published at his press in St. James the first separate history of the straits. His 48 page pamphlet, *Ancient and Modern Michili-mackinac*, appeared in 1854. It went through at least four other Nineteenth Century editions after Strang's assassination by two of his disgruntled followers in 1856.

Popular travel author Bayard Taylor made a brief visit to the island in 1855, and he later recorded his impressions in book form. As his steamer approached he, too, was captivated by the beauty and invigorating air of the straits.

> The surface of the lake was scarcely ruffled by the sweet western wind; the sky was a pale, trans-parent blue, and the shores and islands were as sharply and clearly defined as if carved on a crystal tablet. It was a genuine Northern realm we had entered - no warmth, no depth of color, no un-dulating grace of outline, but bold, abrupt, positive form, cold, pure brilliancy of atmosphere, and an expression of vigor and reality which would make dreams impossible. If there is any air in which action is the very charm and flavor of life, and not its curse, it is the air of Mackinac.

A milestone in the region's promotional annals came that same year when John Disturnell, prominent publisher of travel guides, discovered the island. His *Springs, Water-Falls, Sea Bathing Resorts...and the*

This 1882 view of the docks at Mackinac Island pictures stacks of firewood that fueled steamships.

Most Fashionable Watering-Places, published in 1855, allotted ample space to Mackinac Island, offering an almost irresistable invitation:

Oh ye lovers of fun, and baked, roast, broiled, boiled, grilled, stewed and stuffed peoplers of the deep, just drawn from the flood, this is the place for you. Come and see. Lovers of the wildest profusion nature ever strewed, or a mixture of islands and main, of straits in the sea and stroller on the land, come to the house of *Michabou* - the God of the Lakes - and ye will never turn away, till you have blessed the hour that made you a pilgrim to this land of the fairies.

Two years later Disturnell again boosted Mackinac Island in two separate travel guides, *A Trip Through the Lakes of North America* and *The Upper Lakes of North America.* The latter volume went through numerous revised editions.

In 1857, also, the enthusiastic proprietors of newly platted Mackinaw City commissioned Edward D. Mansfield to write a pamphlet extolling the virtues of what they were convinced was destined to become a "metropolis of the Great Lakes" second only to Detroit. Those investors who were inspired by Mansfield's 48 page promotional tract, depicting a locomotive speeding past a bustling lakeside community, to purchase lots in what remained a city only on paper were doomed to several decades of disappointment. Not until 1871, would Mackinaw City boast even a post office. Only with the arrival of the Grand Rapids and Indiana Railroad in 1881 did the fate of the village seem secure.

The first book-length publication devoted to the straits region, W.P. Strickland's 404 page *Old Mackinaw or the Fortress of the Lakes,* appeared in 1860. It, too, focused on the commercial destiny of

Mackinaw City. Ten years later, the Rev. J.A. Van Fleet published in Ann Arbor the original editon of his popular *Old and New Mackinac.*

In 1870, also, the first of another generation of literary ladies discovered Mackinac Island. Constance Fenimore Woolson began writing numerous magazine articles, short stories and novels about island life. Later, Mary Hartwell Catherwood also authored a series of popular books of fiction set in the straits area.

In 1875 Disturnell issued the first actual tourist-oriented guide book to the straits. That year also marked the success of Mackinac-born Sen. Thomas A. Ferry's efforts to designate the government owned portion of the island as a national park.

Twenty years later the federal government relinquished to the state of Michigan the national park, the military reservation and the fort. Together those tracts became the Mackinac Island State Park. Meanwhile, each succeeding summer brought even more gaping, grasping and galloping hordes of tourists, as generation after generation fell under the lure of Michilimackinac.

The decade of the 1870s marked the 200th anniversary of the first printed description of Michilimackinac. Let us sail away from Mackinac Island's golden era in company with A. Judd Northrup, who spiced his grayling fishing expedition to Northern Michigan with a visit there in 1879:

It was with reluctance - almost with sadness - that we gazed our too early farewell to the historic and romantic island, while we stood on the upper deck and the steamer moved silently out upon the darkening waters and into the evening shades - the steamer's band, meanwhile discoursing strains of music, tranquilizing, tender, soft as the ambiant air or the mirror-like waters beneath.

Depot Dreams & Jerkwater Schemes: Railroad Place-Names in Michigan

The railroad brakeman known only as Barnett fancied himself quite a joker. When the Chicago and West Michigan Railroad pushed its tracks north through Oceana County in 1871 and four local entrepreneurs platted out a village adjacent the new depot, Barnett offered to pay the platting fees if the proprietors would bestow his name on the promising village. The four town fathers accepted his offer, promptly recorded the plat as Barnett and then asked him for the money. Barnett responded that he "was much obliged for the honor conferred upon him but he had only been joking about the fee".

But the last laugh was on the railroad man. Officially, the booming village might be Barnett but none of the locals called it that. To them it was Shelby, the name given the post office and railroad depot. What's more, when civil engineer H.F. Walling compiled his monumental *Atlas of Michigan*, published by R.M. and S.T. Tackabury of Detroit in 1873, he misspelled the town named for the deadbeat brakeman as "Barrett." By the 1884 edition of the atlas, even that had disappeared. The site had become simply Shelby, an appellation it continues to proudly bear.

That fact, however, posed a problem for an Allegan County station on the Grand Rapids and Indiana Railroad also named Shelby in honor of its first station agent. When that community sought a post office in 1872, postal authorities took the liberty of adding "ville" to its name so as not to confuse it with the northern Shelby. So while there continues to be a Shelby and a Shelbyville, there is no Barnett,

Michigan. The moral being: if a man's name is only as good as his word, brakemen who break promises don't get their names on the Michigan map.

Behold that majestic cartographic, the Michigan map. Sprinkled across the peninsulas' grandure lie myriad, musical, magical place-names that perpetuate the state's colorful heritage. Communities bear the names of Chippewa chiefs, French explorers, missionaries, pioneer women, lumbermen, soldiers and statesmen. Some commemorate ancient battles, shipwrecks and the Upper Peninsula's mineral wealth. Still others document the state rich ethnic origins. Few, if any, institution, however, has contributed more to the naming and development of Michigan villages, cities and hamlets than the railroads that whistled away the wilderness.

Behind many of those place-names lies a story worth the telling. Take Rudyard, a Chippewa County community located along the Mackinac Trail, halfway between Sault Ste. Marie and St. Ignace. Created as a station on the Minneapolis, St. Paul & Sault Ste. Marie Railroad in 1887, the depot was originally called Pine River. But when the presence of another Pine River in the Lower Peninsula caused confusion, Fred Underwood, general manager of the railroad and a great admirer of the British poet and chronicler of the "white man's burden," renamed the station Rudyard in 1890.

Underwood chose the poet's first name because three years before he had allotted his surname to another railroad station just north of Gladstone in Delta Country. While Kipling still exists, for some unknown reason it has been taken off the official Michigan transportation map.

Be that as it may, shortly after Underwood had twice decorated the map with the bard's name, a friend informed Kipling of the fact. Whereupon he

The Duluth, South Shore & Atlantic Railroad's crack "The North Country Mail" in 1902.

dashed off:

> "Wise is the child who knows his sire"
>   The ancient proverb ran
> But wiser far the man who knows
>   How, when and where his offspring grows
> For who the mischief would suppose
>   I've sons in Michigan?
>
> Yet am I saved from midnight ills,
>   That weary the souls of man;
> They do not make me walk the floor
>   Nor hammer at the doctor's door,
> They deal in wheat and iron ore,
>   My sons in Michigan.
>
> Oh, tourist in the Pullman car
>   (By Cook's or Raymond's plan)
> Forgive a parent's partial view:
>   But, maybe, you have children, too--
> So let me introduce to you
>   My sons in Michigan.

The poet and novelist who so glorified the British empire is not the only one of its subjects to grace the Upper Peninsula map. In 1884 F.H. Rhinelander, president of the Milwaukee, Lake Shore & Western Railroad, platted and named a village in Gogebic County in honor of Sir Henry Bessemer, the English inventor who discovered the iron smelting process that bears his name. Three years later, William D. Washburn, a prominent Minneapolis flour miller and projector of the Minneapolis, St. Paul & Sault Ste. Marie Railroad, christened a Delta County town after British prime minister, William Evart Gladstone. Not coincidently, that railroad was completed with British capital.

Similar motivation inspired the Chicago and

Northwestern Railroad to transplant English place-names to Upper Peninsula soil in the early 1870s. The railroad changed the Delta County village of Day River to Brampton and named a Menominee County station Kew, now a ghost town, after English cities where its promoters were busy hawking bonds to investors.

While many southern Michigan communities bear the names of New York and New England towns from whence their pioneers came, railroad employees claimed a more cosmopolitan nativity. A Detroit & Mackinac Railroad conductor who hailed from Lachine, Quebec, gave that name to an Alpena County station founded in 1909. Sam Peterson, a homesick railroad agent, renamed the Mackinac County village of Kennedy Siding, Engadine, after a scenic valley in his native Switzerland. That happy circumstance later resulted in a local restaurant labeling itself "The Engadiner."

Not all railroad-inspired place-names boast such exotic derivations. Some were labeled simply because of their location. Communities situated at the intersections of railroads, for example, frequently took the name junction. The Van Buren County village of Grand Junction was platted in 1869 because of its potential at the crossing of the Kalamazoo-South Haven branch of the Michigan Central and the Grand Rapids-Chicago branch of the Pere Marquette railroads. Soo Junction in Luce County sprang up in the 1890s at the joining of the Sault Ste. Marie and St. Ignace branches of the Duluth, South Shore & Atlantic Railroad. Other places such as Grand Trunk Junction in St. Clair County and Junction in Genesee County have disappeared from the map. Another ghost town, Annpere, took its name from its site at the intersection of the Ann Arbor and Pere Marquette railroads.

Other railroad place-names owe their derivation

John M. Ashley built the railroad spur to the village grateful residents named in his honor.

to their use as log loading points during the era when Michigan's commerce in "green gold" led the nation. Chippewa County's Strong's Siding, now simply Strongs, or Strong Corners as the locals refer to it, originated as a place on the Duluth, South Shore & Atlantic Railroad where a Mr. Strong loaded timber. Nowicki Siding, a lumber storage facility in Presque Isle County, while no longer on the map, earned an infamous niche in history as the site of the Metz Fire tragedy where a train load of refugees burned to death in 1908.

Railroad place-namers labeled some towns because of their proximity to existing geographical features. When the Lake Shore & Michigan Southern Railroad came through Allegan County in 1874, it named a depot Hopkins Station simply because of its nearness to Hopkinsburg, with which it did not connect. Hopkins Station, ultimately shortened to Hopkins, thrived, but Hopkinsburg did not. Lake Station, now Lake, in Clare County began as a depot on the Flint & Pere Marquette Railroad in 1877. It was titled such by the railroad because of nearby Crooked Lake. Conversely, Lake George, another Clare County community, on the Toledo, Ann Arbor & Northern Michigan Railroad, took its name not from any aquatic attraction but from its founder, George Lake.

Other railroad inspired place-names appear fanciful at best. A Chicago & Northwestern Railroad official with a taste for classic mythology, for example, dubbed four stations along a twelve mile stretch of the tracks in Menominee County: Dyrads, Faunus, Comus and Hylas. Not unlike their ancient counterparts they are all ghost towns now. The name of another Gladwin County station on the Michigan Central Railroad seemed to presage its fate. The town of Hardluck survived only from 1904 to 1906.

Many a Michigan city, whistle-stop or jerkwater came into being because the railroad chose to stop there. When the Detroit, Grand Haven and Milwaukee Railroad laid tracks through Genesee County in the mid 1850s its depot became the first structure in the incipient village of Gaines. The proprietors of the village of Decatur, platted adjacent the Michigan Central Railroad tracks in Van Buren County in 1847, wisely donated land for the depot the railroad built the following year and thereby insured the survival of the community. The appropriately named Forest began in the early 1870s as a wooding-up stop on the Mackinac Division of the Michigan Central. The Crawford County community ultimately changed its name to Frederic, the first name of its pioneer settler.

When the Grand Rapids and Indiana Railroad established a depot in northern Kent County in the late 1860s, Oscar House platted the village of Edgerton around it. While Edgerton has disappeared from the Michigan map it is fondly remembered by those who cherish truly terrible poetry as the community where Julia Moore, "the sweet singer of Michigan," tended her general store. Julia specialized in odes about the death of young children. Humorist Bill Nye branded the poet "worse than a gatling gun" and suggested her poetic license be revoked. Many of her couplets, rhymed and otherwise, chronicle the sad demise of the once numerous House clan, relatives of Egerton's founder. Julia finished off poor six-year-old Hattie House, who dropped dead amid her playmates, thusly:

> Those little girls will not forget
> The day little Hattie died
> For she was with them
> When she fell in a fit
> While playing by their side.

The Ionia County community of Muir was named in honor of the railroad offical who signed this 1863 advertisement.

If, as we have seen, the presence of a railroad depot could stimulate the birth of a town, for the railroad to miss an existing community might hasten a fate suitable for Moore's most dolorous effusions. When that happened, the citizens of more than one town simply accepted the inevitable and moved their entire community to a site on the railroad. Optimistic entrepreneurs platted an Ionia County town called Bonanza in the late 1870s. But when the Pere Marquette Railroad came through in 1880 and missed Bonanza the townfolk moved it a mile to the southwest and renamed it Lake Odessa. Similarly, when the Pontiac, Oxford and Northern Railroad failed to connect with the Oakland County town of Trombley, the post office was moved a mile and a half south to Leonard, which was on the line, and that was the end of Trombley. Even the ancient community of L'Anse, founded as an Indian mission in 1660, could not resist the power of the railroad. When the builders of the Marquette, Houghton & Ontonagon Railroad bypassed L'Anse, the village center shifted to a new site south of the Lake Superior shore.

Fittingly enough, grateful citizens sometimes named or renamed a village in honor of the official who got the railroad through their locale. Ashley, Bates, Elwell, Lennon and Muir all owe their appellations to such circumstances. Residents of Gates in Tuscola County rewarded the man who won the community a post office and plank road by naming it after him. But when G. W. Reese, superintendent of the Detroit and Bay City Railroad, ran the tracks through the village in 1873, they saw fit to rename it Reese. The villagers at Greene in Saginaw County, on the other hand, rechristened their town Merrill in respect to a railroad superintendent who had befriended them following the devastating forest fire of 1881.

High ranking officials were not the only

railroad employees honored by townsfolk anxious that the iron rails reach their community. The residents of Orient in Osceola County redubbed it Sears in 1870 to honor the surveyor then plotting the route of the Flint & Pere Marquette Railroad. Founded in 1888, the Eaton County village of Mulliken took the name of the contractor who laid the rails that ran through the village.

In 1865 a pair of developers platted out the Barry County village of Nashville which they named for George Nash, the engineer in charge of construction of the Michigan Central Railroad. In appreciation of the honor Nash drew up the plat of the village. Nevertheless, the developers spent a few anxious years since the first train did not come through the village until 1869. Even the boss of a railroad work crew, R. La Rocque, got his name on a Presque Isle County hamlet situated on the Detroit & Mackinaw Railroad in 1895.

Railroad employees frequently took advantage of their knowledge of a planned railroad's route to found communities at likely sites. Michigan Central Railroad Attorney Nathaniel Cheseboro purchased a tract of land and platted out the village of Mattawan in 1845, just prior to the road coming through Van Buren County. No one should have been surprised that the railroad tracks soon neatly bisected the town.

A similar scenario occurred three years later when Nicholas Cheeseborough, a right-of-way buyer for the Michigan Central Railroad, teamed up with Jacob Beeson of Niles, to purchase eighty acres and plat the village of Dowagiac. Edward Powers, a civil engineer for the Chicago and Northwestern Railroad, accomplished an analogous coup in 1872 in Menominee County. He named the resulting town after himself. Imlay City originated in 1870 when Charles Palmer, chief engineer for the Port Huron & Lake Michigan Railroad, looked into his crystal ball

Street Scene, Pullman, Mich.

The Allegan County village of Pullman was named in honor of sleeping car builder George Pullman.

and platted the Lapeer County train station. Within two years it sported a hotel built by Palmer, 15 stores, a grain elevator, sawmill, grist mill and a shingle mill.

Railroad companies also sometimes took advantage of the commercial opportunities their tracks brought and platted towns. The Saginaw & Jackson Railroad, which carried innumerable sportsmen to Michigan's north country, platted a Crawford County community in 1874, naming it Grayling after the famous game fish that once thrived in the cold northern streams. The Milwaukee, Lake Shore & Western Railroad appropriately chose Ironwood as the place-name of the Gogebic County town it created in 1885. The Clare County seat sprang into existence in 1879, when the Flint & Pere Marquette Railroad platted the town along its tracks and generously donated a block for a county court house. The railroad named the site after President William Henry Harrison.

But even such presidential appellations could not endure once a railroad official made up his mind to alter the name of an existing community. The Berrien County village named Lincoln by its founders became Glenlord in 1879 when Monroe N. Lord donated land for the right-of-way of the Chicago & West Michigan Railroad.

Duplication of station names and other factors induced companies to railroad communities into changing their names. As a result, Hoppertown in Allegan County became Pullman, after George Pullman of sleeping car fame. Irvington in Van Buren County became Lacota; Blackwood in Grand Traverse County became Grawn, which sounds like something fish do; and Poverty Nook in Sanilac County became Hemans, after Michigan legislator and historian Lawton T. Hemans.

Most commonly, however, such name alterations honored railroad officials of the line forcing the change. So Hinman in Emmet County became Alanson, Johnsville in Ottawa County became Agnew, Spencer Creek in Antrim County became Alden, and Barnes in Otsego County became Gaylord. In 1870 the Grand River Valley Railroad named a depot it built in southern Kent County, Hammond Station. Later, when the Michigan Central took over the road, it renamed it Dutton for one of its officals.

Railroad conductors found it difficult to pronounce Frankenhilf, a Tuscola County village founded by Bavarian immigrants in 1851. So they simply retitled it Richville, in reference to the surrounding fertile farmland. Occasionally railroads came out on the loosing end of the town-naming game. When the Chicago and West Michigan Railroad came through Berrien County in 1856, it named a station Wilkinson after a family of Virginians who operated a pier and sawmill there. But the U.S. Post Office soon found the southern sympathies of the Wilkinson's unsavory and renamed the community Lakeside for its location.

For lack of a better name railroads sometimes took the expedient of calling stations after their local agent. When the Chicago and Northwestern Railroad was completed from Escanaba to Negaunee in 1865 some of the railroad laborers settled at a site in Delta County later named Lathrop, after Azel Lathrop, the railroad agent there. The Detroit, Hillsdale and Indiana Railroad choose the given name of their resident agent for the Hillsdale County town of Jerome in 1871. Wallace Sutherland, a station agent for the Chicago and Northwestern Railroad also saw his given name perpetuated in a Menominee County community. Chadwick in Ionia County, Doyle in St. Clair County and Hand in Wayne County once honored the surnames of local railroad agents.

But railroads usually reserved such honors for those higher up the corporate ladder. The surnames of

Union Station, Howard City, Mich. ml-13-hcmr

Howard City in Montcalm County honors the name of Detroit railroad attorney William A. Howard.

railroad presidents, directors, superintendents, treasurers and attorneys abound on the Michigan map. They include Baldwin (Delta County), Carland (Shiawassee County), Ewen (Ontonagon County), Faithhorn (Menominee County), Hawks (Presque Isle County), Howard City (Montcalm County), Prescott (Ogemaw County), Wakelee (Cass County), and Wells (Arenac County).

The name of James McMillan, distinguished U.S. senator from Michigan from 1889-1902, is preserved on the map not for his public service, but because he was president of the Detroit, Mackinac & Marquette Railroad when it came through Luce County in 1881. One wonders how George I. Seney, a director of that same railroad, appreciated the honor of his good name being awarded to the community that gained the reputation as one of the nation's worst lumberjack hellholes.

The yearning to spike their monikers on the Michigan map moved some town founders to resort to outright bribery. When the Wabash Railroad came through Lenawee County in 1881 it named a station Balch. Local storekeeper and the community's first postmaster John Britton made numerous lobbying visits to railroad headquarters and ultimately paid $500 before he succeeded in convincing officials to retitle the town after him. Benjamin F. Cooper, a sawmill proprietor in Ottawa County, offered the Detroit, Grand Haven & Milwaukee Railroad all the land it needed if it would only name a station after him in 1858. As a result, Coopersville adorns the Michigan map. Lawton in Van Buren County and the Midland County city of Colman owe their names to similar actions by land donors.

But sometimes such real estate inducements had a way of backfiring. Henry Goss, town founder and first postmaster of the Van Buren County community now known as McDonald, was an eccentric farmer who eschewed shoes from spring to fall. In 1874 he offered the Chicago & West Michigan Railroad land if it would build a depot at his site. The railroad accepted, built the depot and according to local lore, first called the station Barefoot in his honor.

Other more modest town namers relinquished the personal honor in favor of a loved one. A Toledo & Ann Arbor Railroad executive renamed Reeves Station in Monroe County after his daughter Azelia. Fred H. May of Allegan, general manager of the short-lived Grand Haven Railroad, named a Muskegon County resort community founded in 1880 after the apple of his eye, daughter Mona May. In 1889, James M. Ashley, one of the builders of the Ann Arbor Railroad through Wexford County, platted a village he named Harriette, an amalgamation of the names of his father, Harry, and fiancee Henriette Burt. But two years later the village was incorporated as Gaston. Ashley promptly threatened to close the station unless the original name was retained. Needless to say, Harriette it remained although the spelling ultimately became Harrietta. H.C. Potter, general manager of the Flint & Pere Marquette Railroad, sought to insure marital bliss by naming a Clare County station Farwell after his father-in- law.

Love of his spouse, or fear, inspired at least one other town namer. In 1868, James L. Bush platted an Isabella County village originally known as Halfway He offered the Ann Arbor Railroad free land for a depot if they would only name the station Rosebush after his beloved wife's maiden name, Rosebush, and it agreed. A few years later, however, when Elias B. Calkins platted an addition to the village he named after himself the post office became Calkinsville. Freight was routed to Rosebush but the mail came to Calkinsville. The rival namers battled for cartographic immortality over the following three decades with the post office changing from Calkinsville to Rosebush and then back to Calkinsville. Finally in 1903 the community permanently became Rosebush.

> "What's in a name?
> That which we call a rose,
> By any other name,
> would smell as sweet;"

Or, with apologies to Gertrude Stein, a Rosebush is a Rosebush is a Rosebush.

Laurence of Superior:
How A Scot Saw the Sault in 1854

"Save the man with the red hair!," yelling frantically, the gambler raced toward the crowd of spectators thronging the St. Marys River shore. "Save the man with the red hair!," he shouted. Thrashing helplessly amid the boiling white water were two tourists who had foolishly attempted to shoot the raging rapids in a canoe without a requisite Indian steersman. As the swift current swept them by, there seemed nothing anyone could do but watch.

Galvanized into action by that desperate appeal, several of the onlookers managed to drag the nearly drowned redhead to shore. "He owes me $18," explained the wide-eyed gambler to anyone who would listen. His unfortunate canoeing partner, however, who apparently had no creditors at the Sault, "paid his debt to nature."

It was a midsummer's day in 1854 when British adventurer, writer and then Canadian Indian agent Laurence Oliphant heard that story from a witness to the event. The narrator then proceeded to draw a moral from the incident - "a man'll never know how necessary he is to society if he don't make his life valuable to his friends as well as to his self."

Throughout the 19th Century many distinguished Europeans toured the Upper Peninsula. Of those who recorded their experiences in book form few led as flamboyant lives or wrote in such a colorful manner as Oliphant. The son of a Scottish lawyer, Oliphant was born in 1829, in Cape Town, South Africa, where his father was serving as attorney general. For health reasons his mother returned to the ancestral estate in Perthshire and took her son with her. In typical British fashion, he received his education at a private boarding school, seeing his mother only during vacations. When the elder Oliphant was knighted and appointed chief justice of Ceylon, the family joined him there in 1841. His father returned to Europe on a two year leave in 1846 and the family took an extended continental tour, visiting France, Germany, the Alps, Italy and Greece. While in Italy young Oliphant witnessed the street fighting that marked the beginning of the Italian War of Independence from Austria. Returning to Ceylon, he served as his father's private secretary and he also became a lawyer. By the time he was 22 his practice had included 23 murder cases.

In 1851, Oliphant accompanied an Indian raja on a hunting expedition to Nepal, which he described in his first book, *A Journey to Khatmandu* (1852). Oliphant continued his whirlwind travels whenever and wherever opportunity permitted. His second book appeared in 1853, *The Russian Shores of the Black Sea in the Autumn of 1852, and a Tour Through the Country of the Don Cossacks*. The outbreak of the Crimean War helped make that volume a best seller and its young author served as a consultant to Lord Raglan prior to his campaign against the Russians.

Another opportunity for travel and adventure came in 1853 when the governor general of Canada, James Bruce, offered him an appointment as his secretary. He assisted him in Washington during the negotiation of the Canadian Reciprocity Treaty of 1854 that settled a long standing fishing rights dispute. Back in Quebec, Bruce appointed Oliphant superintendent of Indian affairs. As part of his responsibilities he launched his tour to the Lake Superior country with a companion cited only as "B."

It was a bright August day when their ship steamed up the St. Marys River. Oliphant stood on deck, peering through his telescope at the American

113

Sault. At first glance he thought it quite an imposing city:

> Substantial looking houses line the water's edge; and as the site upon which the city is built is almost perfectly level, it has the appearance of indefinite extent. There were flags flying to denote hotels, and upon the only rising ground in the neighborhood the stars and strips were floating also to denote Yankee supremacy, for it was crowned by a neat whitewashed stockaded fort.

The small Hudson's Bay Company fort and the straggling houses surrounding it on the Canadian side seemed so cheerless to Oliphant compared to Fort Brady and the bustling American Sault that he decided to "sacrifice patriotism to comfort." A half hour after the ship docked on the Canadian side, Oliphant and companion had crossed the river in a ferry, landing "at a rickety wooden pier, passing between two high wooden houses." His first impression of the Sault, that it was a metropolis, was soon dashed when he discovered the entire city stretched along a single road, Water Street.

Oliphant observed wooden houses with their gables to the street, at least one of which still stands on the south side of Water Street and:

> A large dry goods store, then a newspaper office, (the *Lake Superior Journal* which relocated to Marquette in 1855), then the Metropolitan saloons, next to that Hopkins saloon, then a bowling saloon, and the Paris store; in fact, to judge from the great number of houses of entertainment in proportion to those of other character, the town seemed to be nothing more or less than a large tavern with a shop at the back.

The Chippewa House as it appeared in 1889.

Sault Ste. Marie in 1854 was a rip-roaring frontier river town catering to hordes of sailors, copper and iron miners on holiday, Irish laborers digging the Sault Canal, voyageurs, Indians, tourists looking for exciting times - and cheap liquor flowed like water. Oliphant had not been the first visitor to the Sault to note the inordinate number of barrooms.

J. Elliot Cabot, a member of Louis Agassiz's scientific expedition to Lake Superior stopped briefly at the Sault in 1848. He observed:

> The most striking feature of the place is the number of dramshops and bowling alleys. Standing in front of one of the hotels I counted seven buildings where liquor was sold, besides the larger stores; where this was only one article among others. The roar of bowling alleys and the click of billiard balls are heard from morning until late at night. The whole aspect is that of a western village on the fourth of July afternoon. Nobody seems to be at home, but all out on a spree or going fishing or bowling... Nobody is busy but the barkeepers...

Oliphant was not quite as critical of the situation he found at the Sault as was the Boston bluenose. Indeed, during the several days he spent there waiting for the arrival of the *Sam Ward* to carry him westward, he quite enjoyed the bowling bars in the evening.

Oliphant and his companion soon checked into the Chippewa House, a rambling hotel that stood on the southeast corner of Water Street and Ashmun Avenue until it burned to the ground in 1896. After bathing and donning clothes "most likely to create an impression;" the two sallied forth to see the Sault. In contrast to the "rough and uncouth" appearance of the town, the British travelers were surprised to encounter a group of cultured Eastern sportsmen discussing the day's hunting and fishing adventures while lounging in tilted chairs on the long veranda that stretched across the front of the hotel. Stylishly dressed in "evening coats and patent leather boots or velveteen shooting coats, with their trousers tucked inside neat Wellington boots," the gentlemen welcomed the British to the Sault, informing them "its quite a pleasurable locality."

The tourism that would ultimately comprise a dominant part of the Upper Peninsula's economy might be in its infancy elsewhere, but the Sault had already become a fashionable resort that Oliphant found "full of Americans from all parts of the northern states, who make summer excursions to Lake Superior, and who patronize the Sault largely as a sort of watering place, with the advantage of sport in the shape of (passenger) pigeons and trout in the neighborhood."

While they stood conversing on the veranda, the hotel dinner bell rang and the sportsmen made a sudden rush for the dining room. The American taste for fast food, it seems, had already become a well established cultural phenomenon. Oliphant and companion, who soon discovered they were novices in the art of dining in the backwoods, leisurely strolled to the large dining room. There, they found at least 150 people already seated, "the ladies and the gentlemen with ladies, having the privilege of private entry before the bell rings."

Unlike modern restaurants, hotel dining rooms of that era featured boarding house type meals, where, amid great pandamonium, guests ate as much as they could as fast as they could or went without. The British managed to secure seats at a table on the fringe "which was perfectly destitute of food, nor did it seem likely that we should get any, for everyone else was too busy engaged even to talk, while any attempt at conversation would have been drowned in the clatter of knives and forks." They finally succeeded in getting a little something to eat, reconciling themselves that "it had been swallowed with a rapidity which would have rendered any increase in quantity productive of serious results."

During a later meal on the frontier Oliphant timed the proceedings and found that "from the moment when the first rush into the dining room took place, to the moment when the first man left it, was exactly seven minutes and a half. In ten minutes I remained the solitary spectator of a melancholy array of empty dishes, the contents of which had been sufficient, in that short period, to satisfy nearly a hundred voracious denizens of the far west."

Adventures in dining, drinking and bowling were not the only allurements the British travelers found at the Sault. They toured Fort Brady, a white palisaded containment then located at the water's edge near the present site of the River of History Museum, and the Hudson's Bay Company fort on the Canadian side. They observed the bustling construction work being done on the canal and locks, and they spent many hours shopping for supplies that would be unavailable farther west. And like many another tourist before and after, until construction of a compensating dam tamed the furious rapids, they experienced the carnival ride thrills of shooting the Sault Rapids in a birch bark canoe. Unlike the red-headed man and his unfortunate passenger they wisely hired two local voyageurs. Oliphant described that memorable ride:

Seating ourselves steadily at the bottom of our frail bark canoe, we allowed it to be sucked into the foaming waters, a voyageur at each end of the canoe, with quick eye and strong arms, prepared to steer us safely upon a voyage which certainly, to

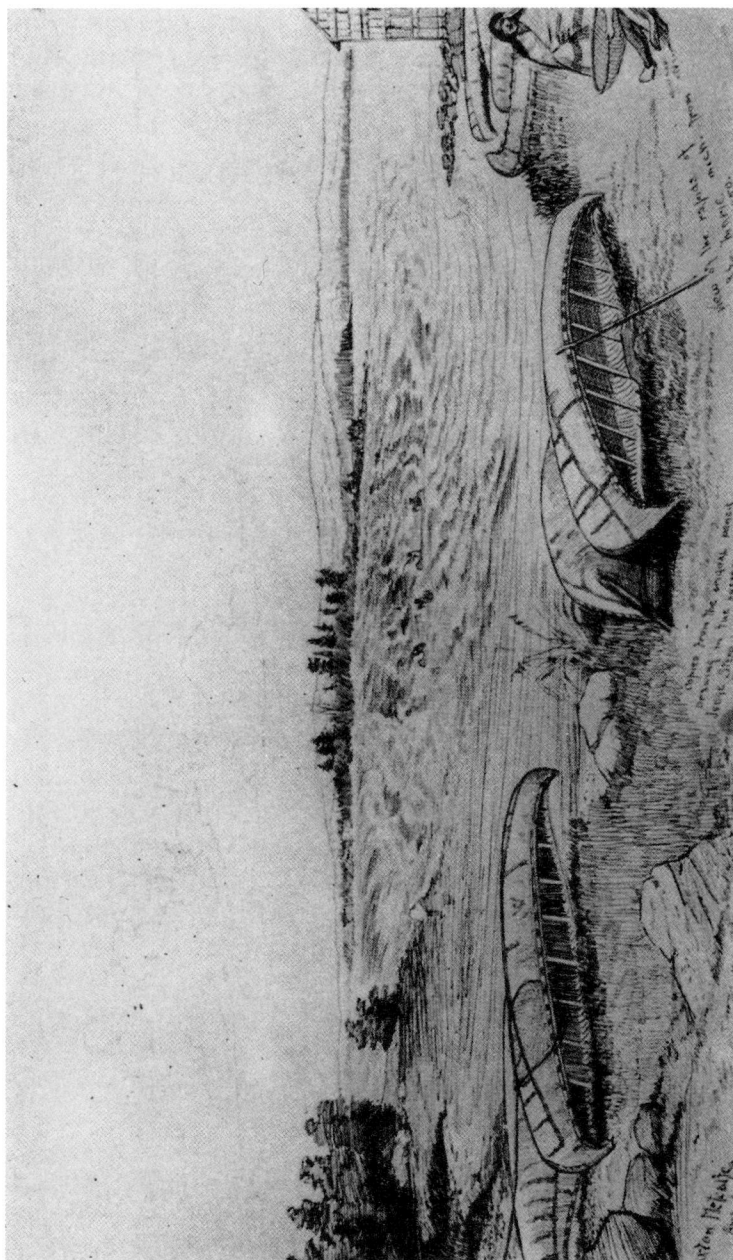

The furious St. Marys Rapids, sketched by Wharton Metcalf in 1850.

the uninitiated, did not seem altogether devoid of peril. The surface of the river over an extent of at least a mile square, presents at this point one unbroken sheet of foam. The waves are so high that they dash into the canoe, which would inevitable be upset if, by bad steering, it were allowed to get into the trough of the sea. We were just beginning to acquire a fearful velocity, when, as if to harmonize with the tumult of waters amid which we were being so widely tossed, vivid flashes of lightening burst forth from the black clouds, followed by loud peals of thunder, and rendered the descent of these rapids, which is always exciting, grand and almost appalling, In about four minutes we were in smooth water again, having in that period accomplished a distance which it had taken an hour to traverse on our upward course.

A thrilling tourist attraction as well as famous fishing grounds where the local Chippewa dexterously netted huge whitefish, the boulder-strewn Sault Rapids, over which the furious waters of the St. Marys River drop 18 feet in a half mile, also posed an impassable barrier to shipping on the only water route into Lake Superior. The summer before Oliphant's visit, Charles T. Harvey had begun construction of the engineering marvel that would unlock the mineral riches of the Upper Peninsula. His army of Irish construction workers, two to three thousand strong, would succeed in blasting and hand chiseling through solid rock a 5,400 foot canal equipped with two 350 foot locks. But until the Sault Canal opened on June 18, 1855, supplies and minerals were transported around the rapids on a primitive strap iron railroad. Cargo was laboriously unloaded into tram cars and pulled by horses, men and mules over a mile on tracks that ran along the present day Water and Portage streets.

Oliphant thought that tram road the "most characteristic feature of the Sault." He marveled at the rumbling cars loaded with great chunks of pure Keweenaw copper, some more than three tons in weight.

On the morning of his departure from the Sault, Oliphant was startled to find that mineral freight had been displaced by luggage and "seated in picturesque attitudes upon piles of boxes and carpet bags, about 200 persons were waiting to be trundled away to the steamer." With the eye of an artist Oliphant described his motley fellow passengers:

Fragile, delicate-looking ladies, with pink and white complexions, black ringlets, bright dresses, and thin satin shoes, reclined gracefully upon carpet bags, and presided over pyramids of band boxes. Square built German fraus sat astride huge rolls of bedding, displaying stout legs, blue waisted stockings, and hob-nailed shoes. Sallow Yankees, with straw hats, swallow-tailed coats, and pumps, carried their little all in their pockets; and having nothing to lose and everything to gain in the western world to which they were bound, whittled, smoked, or chewed cheerfully. Hard featured, bronzed miners, having spent their earnings in the bowling saloons at the Sault, were returning to the bowels of the earth gloomily. There were tourists in various costumes, doing the agreeable to the ladies, and hardy pioneers of the woods, in flannel shirts and trousers supported by leather belts, and well supplied with bowies, were telling tough yarns, and astonishing the weak minds of the emigrants who represented half the countries of Europe.

Every available spot on the long line of cars

Strap railroad tracks dominated Sault Ste. Marie's Water Street in 1850.

being covered with this colorful mass of human freight, Oliphant was hard pressed to find a seat. Finally "a thin man, with high cheek bones, and a red beard" invited him to share the top of a barrel. Scrambling upon it, Oliphant lit a cigar, and offered one to his new friend, when with horror he noticed some little black "suspious looking" grains jostling up through a crack in the lid. They were seated on a barrel of blasting powder! Springing off, Oliphant seized his companion's hand just in time to stop him from lighting up a "fresh fusee." The man casually swung down remarking "he had come darned near bursting up the crowd." After that close call the two decided they would walk the mile to where their steamer, the *Sam Ward*, awaited.

Built in Newport, Michigan, in 1847, the 433 ton side-wheeler, had been laboriously portaged around the rapids on greased logs earlier that year. Though it was crowded with nearly 300 passengers, Oliphant thought the *Sam Ward* large and roomy and he enjoyed comfortable accommodations. Steaming westward, toward evening the ship entered the "broad bosom" of Whitefish Bay. By the next morning they had reached the Pictured Rocks, passing them at too great a distance to fully appreciate their majesty. Oliphant saw enough, however, to predict that "people from all parts of the world will make the Pictured Rocks a favorite resort."

He should have quit gazing into his crystal ball with that prediction. His next prognostication, that it was doubtful that Lake Superior iron ore would "ever be able to compete with that of Lake Champlain or New Jersey," cast considerable doubt on his prophetic abilities.

The *Sam Ward* docked at Marquette, where Oliphant had two hours to ramble about the community that had been established but five years previously. He thought Marquette a delightful

Founded in 1849, Marquette was originally called Worchester.

watering place with "a very respectable hotel always full during the summer of pleasure or health seeking Yankees." He described the village as "embossomed in wood, which reaches to the water's edge; rocky promontories jut far into the lake; and enterprising pine trees shoot up between the crevices, and overshadow the deep clear water, with the white sand sparkling at the bottom... The whole forms an enchanting picture, the background to which is composed of a range of wooded hills about 1,000 feet in height."

Leaving Marquette, The *Sam Ward* churned north toward the tip of the Keweenaw Peninsula. Even when there was no scenery to be observed life on board that floating palace was not devoid of interest. Oliphant and his companion occupied a state room adjoining the cabin of the captain, who he described as "the most hospitable and jovial of inland navigators." The state room opened on a balcony, where "at all hours was collected a noisy group, taking what they called 'nips,' smoking mahogany-tinted meerschaums or fragrant havanahs, with a standard rule that each member of the party should furnish a story, a song, or a bottle of wine." Other diversions included endless games of euchre, seven-up and poker where "considerable sums changed hands" and evening dances featuring guitar and fiddle tunes played by black musicians who worked as ship's barbers during the day.

Passing between Keweenaw Point and Manitou Island just as the sun was setting, the *Sam Ward* docked briefly at Copper Harbor to allow some miners to disembark. Oliphant thought it a "pretty village, containing five or six hundred inhabitants situated at the head of a deep landlocked bay, where the neat white houses contrasted strongly with the somber pine woods that overshadowed them." The ship proceeded down the coast to Eagle Harbor and

Eagle River, where at the nearby Cliff Mine, Oliphant learned, a mass of solid copper weighing 160 tons was being laboriously hand-chiseled into manageable pieces.

The *Sam Ward* made its last Michigan stop at Ontonagon. Most of the passengers made a beeline for the barroom of the local hotel, operated by the community's first settler, James Kirk Paul. Oliphant described the hotel as "a most capacious structure, not quite completed, but it looked worthy of a great nation, as it towered above the log shanties which surrounded it."

Rather than join his fellow travelers busy "liquoring up" at the bar, Oliphant explored the community. After settling there in 1843, Paul had begun platting Ontonagon, filing the plat the same year as Oliphant's visit. Oliphant described it as:

A perfect specimen of a backwood town in an embryo state. Stumps still stood in the principal streets, and the old forest still seemed to dispute the soil with the settlers. There had been no time to cut down trees or underwood which did not positively impede communication. Occasionally a living tree formed the upright at the corner of a house, while its companions had been felled and piled upon one another for walls. Sometimes a house was built upon half-a-dozen stumps five or six feet above the ground. The object of the builder seemed not to be permanency, but shelter at any price; and to obtain it, he availed himself of every natural assistance. Then, almost before he had a roof over his head, he entered upon a miscellaneous business. There are Yankee notions of every description in the front window, and a bowling alley at the back. He carries on his profession as a lawyer in his bedroom, sells cutlery and dry goods across his counter, and occupies his leisure moments with medicine. There is a bar connected with the alley, where he dispenses slings, juleps and cobblers, behind which there are stores of all sorts, - pork, flour, tobacco, etc. Upon the other side of the street he is erecting a solid mansion with the proceeds of his present lucrative business, and having landed only two months ago from the *Sam Ward*, without a darned cent in his pocket, is already deeply involved in mining transactions, and expects to make and lose five fortunes in the course of as many years, when his present location will have become too crowded, and he'll "clar out," to go through a similar experience elsewhere.

From Ontonagon the *Sam Ward* steamed to La Pointe and Fond du Lac, where Oliphant and his companion bid adieu to comfortable travels. They proceeded by voyageur canoe to the headwaters of the Mississippi, then down the river and overland to Chicago. There they climbed aboard a train for a fast ride across southern Michigan and on to Niagara Falls and Canada.

Late in 1854 Oliphant resigned his position as superintendent of Indian affairs and returned to England. But not for long. A few months later he was off for the Crimean War front, the siege of Sebastopol and the Circassian Coast. Next he served as a newspaper correspondent with the Turkish army under Omar Pasha. Returning to England, he wrote another book describing his experiences. The year 1856 found him back in America, touring the South. At New Orleans he joined William Walker's ill-fated filibustering expedition to Nicaragua, "partly for the fun of the thing." At the mouth of the San Juan River, the expedition encountered a British warship, and her captain boarded Oliphant's vessel and removed him as a British subject.

The next few years found Oliphant hopping about the globe to wherever conflicts erupted: China, India, Korea, Poland, Hong Kong and Italy, where he engaged in a plot with Garibaldi. He served as a diplomat to Japan in 1861. During a night attack on the embassy, Oliphant rushed out, armed only with a riding whip, and was severely wounded by a Samurai assassin. He survived only because a beam, invisible in the darkness, blocked the sword blows. Retiring from the diplomatic service, Oliphant continued to ramble and write. He settled down briefly in 1865, winning election to Parliament.

During his adventurous career, Oliphant also became interested in occult religions, dabbling in spiritualism. He came under the sway of Thomas Lake Harris, a charismatic prophet who cast out devils and formed magnetic circles among his followers. In 1867 Oliphant resigned his seat in Parliament and he and his mother joined Harris's socialist community near the Lake Erie town of Brockton, New York.

Oliphant became Harris's "spiritual slave," signing over all his assets to the master. To regenerate him, Harris had him clean stables, carry water and other humiliating tasks, and he forbid him to communicate with his mother. In 1870 Harris allowed Oliphant to return to Europe with the understanding that he would be summoned back by a sign - a bullet entering his room. While covering the Franco-Prussian War as a front line correspondent first with the French and then the German army, the sign came - a stray bullet creased his hair. He promptly returned to the prophet.

The following year he again returned to Europe where he met and fell in love with beautiful 26-year-old Alice LeStrange. Harris withheld his permission for a marriage for some time, until Alice agreed to sign over all her property to him. They married in 1872, but the following year Harris ordered Oliphant's wife and

Harper's Weekly ran this woodcut of Oliphant following his
death in 1888.

mother back to Brockton, and assigned him else-where. Not long after, Harris migrated to Santa Rosa, California, and took Alice with him. Oliphant was forbidden to see her. Not until the death of his mother in 1881 and their subsequent loss of faith in the master would Oliphant be fully reconciled with his wife.

They spent the next five years in relative happiness, living at the Brockton estate, where Oliphant had succeeded Harris as leader, writing occult books together and traveling. Oliphant also became involved in a scheme to establish a Jewish colony in Palestine. When Alice died of a fever contracted during a trip to Palestine in 1887, Oliphant returned to England, a broken man.

In 1888 he married a medium, the daughter of Hoosier socialist, spiritualist and social reformer Robert Dale Owen, so that he could communicate with his beloved Alice. A few days after the marriage he grew ill and four months later he died at the age of 59.

Oliphant had packed a lot into his short life-adventures, world travels, military experiences, politics, numerous published books. The promise of his early career had unfortunately given way to unhappiness via religious delusion. But let us leave this fascinating figure not in tragedy but in the bright days of youth aboard the *Samuel Ward,* steaming along the Michigan shoreline of Lake Superior. The evening dance has begun and Oliphant has spied a dark-eyed, raven-haired beauty. Making his way closer, trying to get up the courage to ask her to dance, with "a thrill of pleasure" he hears her remark "that she had a mind to take the knots out of her legs." Taking that cue, he requests the honor of escorting her to the dance floor - but let Oliphant describe what happened next:

Alas! I little knew what I had undertaken, or how completely I had over estimated my own saltatory powers. Our *vis-a-vis* were a very tall, thin, flat lady, with a figure like a plank, and a short wizened old man, who reached to her elbow, with grey bushy eyebrows, which almost concealed his small piercing eyes, and a huge grizzly beard, so thick and matted, that when he compressed his lips, in the energy of the dance, it was impossible to tell within a quarter of an inch where his mouth was. During the moments of rest, however, he twitched it with a short jerking motion, as if he was knitting with his jaws. He was buttoned up to the chin in a straight military looking coat, but he had short baggy trousers, dirty stockings and his large splay feet were thrust into a pair of very old pumps.

The band played Negro melodies and accompanied themselves vocally. The dance was a sort of cotillion; but we were entirely dependent for our figures upon the caprice of the band leader who periodically shouted his orders. My partner and the little old man opposite commenced operations. With clenched teeth and contracted brow did he give himself up to the pleasures of the dance. Now he plunged violently forward, then retreated with a sort of jig step, then seized my partner by the waist, and whirling her rapidly into the middle, danced round her demoniacally, then pirouetted first on one leg, then on the other, then jumped into the air with both, then retired breathless to scowl at me and work his jaws defiantly.

As my turn came I now made a dash at his partner, and attempted a series of similar gymnastic exercises, in a solemn and violent way, conscious all the while of the glance of profound contempt with which my fair companion eyed my performances, as I energetically hopped round her tall *vis-a-vis*, whom I might have imagined a Maypole. But not until the dance became more complicated, and the orders followed each other with rapidity, and distracted my attention, did I feel the full effect of my rashness.

The band sang, "Heigh Nelly, Ho Nelly, listen lub to me;" and then the leader shouted, "Gents to the right!" and away we all shot in the required directions. Then came, "I sing for you - I play for you a dulcem melody." "Balance in line!" There was a puzzle. I got into everybody's line but my own; and my partner, with her sweet smile said that "I had come near riling her;" so that I was much relieved when the last order came of "promenade all to your seats;" and in a state of extreme exhaustion we threw ourselves on a couch, satisfied that the great end had been gained, and that no knot could have been obstinate enough to resist such violent treatment.

Celebrated Celery City Quacks

It was the golden age of quackery, and Victorian sufferers swallowed massive doses of medical humbuggery along with their alcohol-laden elixirs. Kalamazoo, then popularly known as the Celery City, offered a full complement of colorful cures. Local newspapers and magazines teemed with advertisements promising relief from "lost manhood," "nervous weakness," "diseases peculiar to women" and every other conceivable dangerous or embarrassing affliction. Scores of opportunistic druggists, self-styled doctors and businessmen-turned-charlatans compounded the likes of Harrison's Hair Hastener, Odell's Wonderful Oil, the Great Catarrh Annihilator and Kill-All-Hair treatment. Other apparently genuine and trustworthy Kalamazoo entrepreneurs greeted drugstore patrons from the labels of Zoa-Phora, Tuberculozyne and an array of celery-flavored sex stimulants.

As if to further confound the clientele, local physicians hung their shingles under the guise of a bewildering variety of medical theories. In contrast to "regular doctors," homeopaths administered drugs that caused a healthy person to develop symptoms similar to the patient's complaint. Allopaths' prescriptions, on the other hand, sought to produce effects different from those brought about by the disease being treated. And eclectics chose freely from both beliefs. Pseudoscientific practitioners energetically advocated hydrotherapy, magnetism, clairvoyance and naturopathy. Doctor S.E. Morrill, the female medical electrician, jolted her patients back to health, and Mrs. C.H. Stimpson prescribed Opaline Suppositories as a cure-all. Quacks and regular doctors alike routinely diagnosed fearful-sounding diseases - the ague, catarrh, salt rheum, La Grippe, night sweats, lung chills and galloping consumption. Meanwhile,

133

diphtheria, typhoid fever and dysentery killed hundreds.

As Kalamazoo's economy boomed in the late nineteenth century, self-educated inventors and businessmen on the make marketed products calculated to fill the new needs of the industrial era. While some local entrepreneurs made fortunes via cigars, carriages, caskets and corsets, others took advantage of the government's laissez faire regulatory policy to enter the lucrative field of patent medicines.

Actually, the bottled nostrums loosely referred to as patent medicines are more correctly called proprietary medicines, since few were patented. After seventeen years a patent became part of the public domain, but registered brands and trademarks, a type of copyright, could be renewed every twenty years. Moreover the name was usually more important than the contents, anyway.

The United States Indian Commission forbade the sale of patent medicines to its wards. Such medicines seemed to have the same effect as "firewater." Small wonder: their alcoholic content ran as high as 48 percent (equivalent to 96 proof whiskey), and most contained at least 20 percent alcohol. Instructions directing sufferers to drink as much as three wine glasses full in 45 minutes assured at least a temporary lessening of pain.

Not that Kalamazooans of the Gay Nineties were unfamiliar with the traditional joys of alcohol. Drunkenness was the major offense committed by the 489 miscreants who took a ride in the city's newly acquired paddy wagon in 1890. Tipplers might choose from nearly fifty saloons, half of them packed along the five blocks of Main Street that composed the heart of the city. But those who did not want to sully their good names by appearing in taverns and those who preached temperance could swig medicine

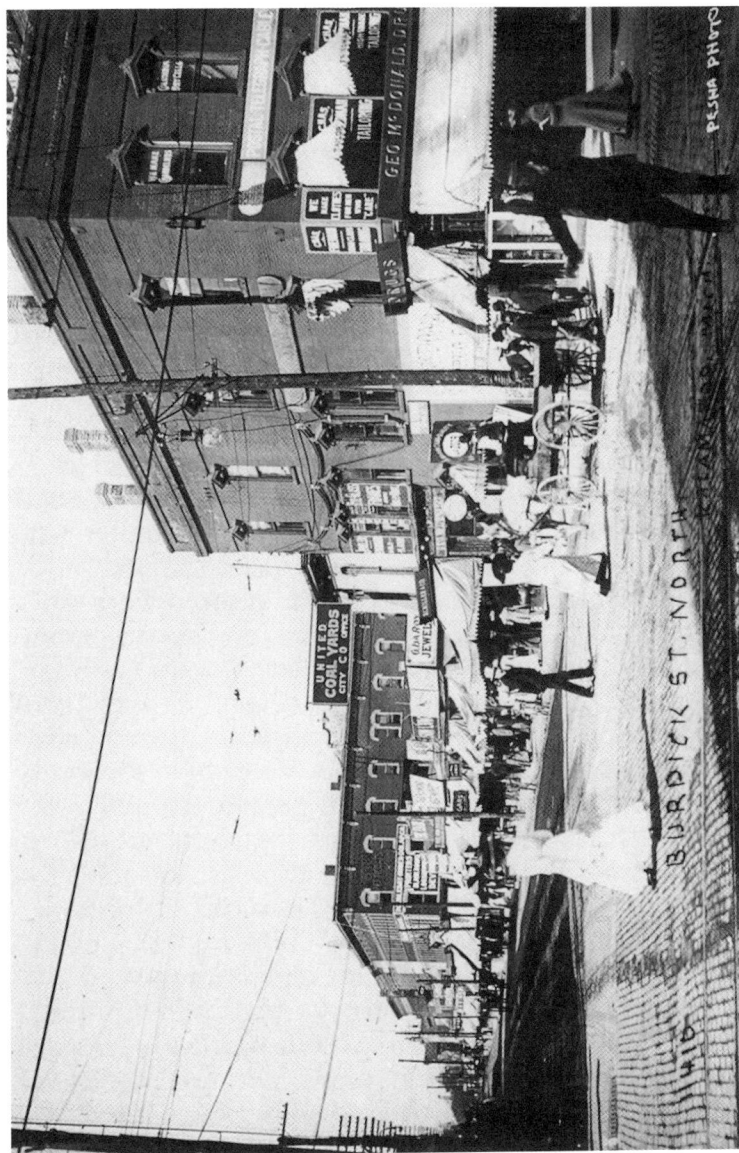

Turn-of-the-century Kalamazoo boasted numerous medical scams.

with a clear conscience.

Kalamazoo was most famous, however, for neither its taverns nor its manufactured products, but for a familiar garden vegetable - celery. By the 1890s some 350 celery growers cultivated over 4,000 swampy acres of muck, making Kalamazoo Township the nation's leading celery-growing district. Banqueters across the country chewed Kalamazoo celery, and vendors hawking huge stalks of the crunchy vegetable startled travelers stopping at the city's Michigan Central train depot.

Victorians found many imaginative uses for celery, most based on a popular belief in its nerve-quieting qualities. At ornate drugstore soda fountains Kalamazooans consumed tall glasses of cooling celery phosphate, petite helpings of creme de celeri and mugs of hot ox celery (celery seed essence and extract of beef). James Farnum, a Portage Avenue retailer who specialized in the rather incongruous combination of wood, coal and celery, also manufactured Farnum's Famous Kalamazoo Celery and Pepsin Chewing Gum. The Kalamazoo Soap Company made Celery Tar Soap, and Samuel J. Dunkley, a local celery shipper, produced canned celery, celery pepper and celery pickles with limited success. Dunkley's Celeryade Drops, a quasi-medicinal candy, achieved greater acceptance.

Nationwide, scores of patent medicine manufacturers put up celery-based nostrums good for that rather nebulous category, "nervous disorders." They included Celery Bitters, Viburnated Celery, Celerena, Celery Cola, Paine's Celery Compound and Sears and Roebuck's Celery Malt Compound. Though advertising emphasized celery's nerve-quieting reputation, most manufacturers took the added precaution of bracing the solution with 20 to 40 percent alcohol.

Kalamazoo medicine manufacturers certainly did not waste the Celery City's good name. The P.L.

SEVEN   SEVENTEEN   SEVENTY

USE CELERY TONIC AND BITTERS.

At Seven! a sly kiss is so sweet,
To steal one now and then's a treat.

At Seventeen! they're nicer still,
And there's a way where there's a will.

At Seventy! it's just the same,
They still keep up the old, old game.

ONE OF THESE PHOTOS SENT TO ANY ADDRESS ON RECEIPT OF THREE TWO CENT STAMPS.   ADDRESS CELERY MEDICINE CO., KALAMAZOO, MICH.

The Celery Medicine Company's trade card promoted the sexual power of celery.

137

Abbey Company, "Manufacturing Pharmacists," made a specialty of celery preparations at their 11,000-square-foot building on Walbridge Street. Until a disastrous fire in 1898 put them out of business, the Hall Brothers produced Celery Compound, which contained celery and catnip, and Celerine Compound, which contained in an alcohol base, celery seeds, black haw, kola nuts and coca leaves (the source of cocaine). The Kalamazoo Medicine Company concocted Kalamazoo Celery Pepsin Bitters, and the Quality Drug Stores marketed Kalamazoo Celery and Sarsaparilla Compound as a cure for "fever and ague, all forms of nervousness, headache, and neuralgia," and a "positive cure for female complaints." Though the federal government later fined the Quality Drug Stores for fraudulent advertising, few consumers complained. A belt of Celery Compound laced with 40 percent alcohol certainly seemed to improve or at least cheer up a "nervous disposition" - or maybe it was the catnip.

Other Kalamazoo entrepreneurs emphasized celery's other folk medicine attribute -that it was an sex stimulant. In 1895 the Celery Medicine Company, located in the 300 block of East Michigan, offered its Celery Tonic Bitters as "the only true nerve tonic and appetizer." The company's trade cards pictured three sets of amorous couples aged seven, seventeen and seventy with the poetic explanation:

> At seven: A sly kiss is so sweet,
> To steal one now and then's a treat.
> At seventeen: they're nicer still'
> And there's a way where there's a will.
> At seventy: it's just the same
> They still keep up the old, old game.

A few years later Samuel J. Dunkley abandoned his celery pickles and celery candy to

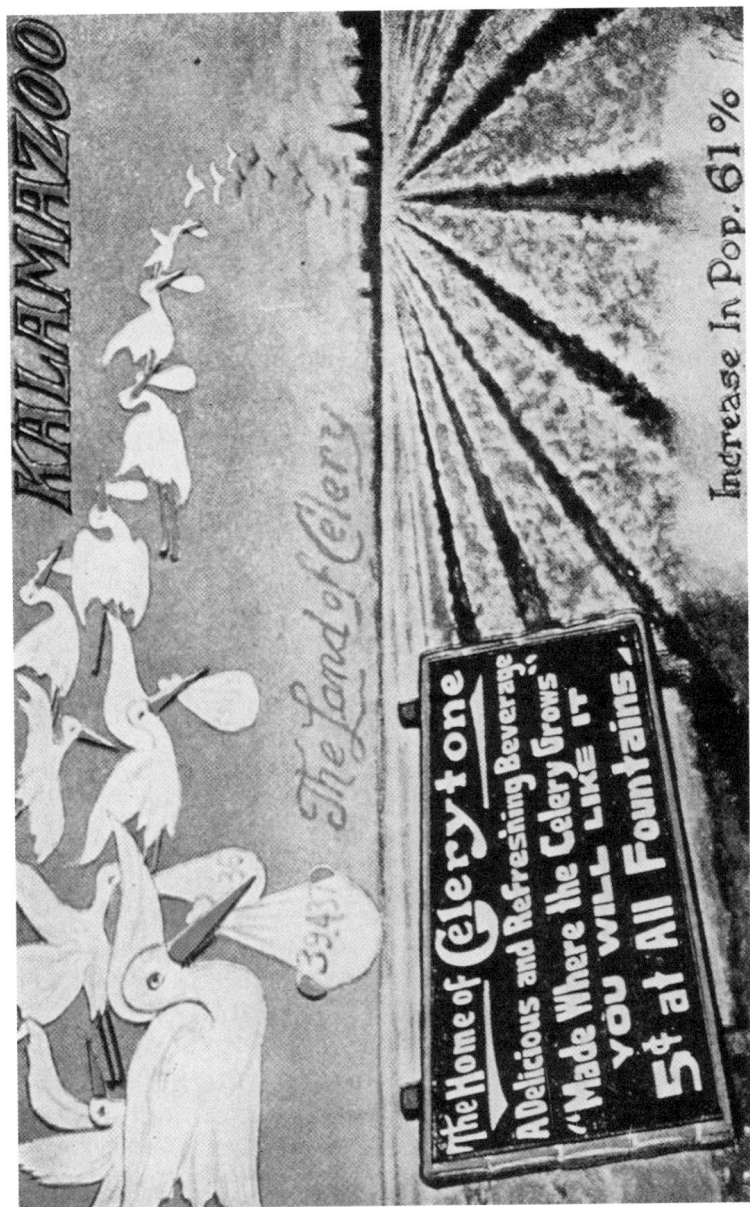

Use of Samuel J. Dunkley's Celerytone promised the imminent arrival of the stork.

concoct the area's most blatant sexual elixir, Celerytone. Dunkley distributed as an advertising premium a series of postcard-size views of the gamboling chubby nudes that Victorians relished - the "Celerytone Nude in Art Miniature Series." Subliminally suggestive advertising guaranteed that only "silver white celery juices" were used. A more straightforward message promised that "the beneficial effect of the peculiar properties of celery upon the nervous and sexual system is wonderful and unequaled. It strengthens exhausted nature, and rejuvenates the entire being, counteracts dissipation, etc. if you get genuine Celerytone."

While the nervous gulped celery tinctures, or chewed celery gum, women in need of similar bolstering sipped Kalamazoo's most famous medicinal cure, Zoa-Phora, Greek for "the health bringer." The Rev. Richard Pengelly, M.D., put forth his first bottle of the remedy he called "Dr. Pengelly's Women's Friend" about the year 1871. Like "most other throughbred physicians" he had valiantly resisted entering the field of patent medicines, until then. Based on the wisdom learned over many years of alleviating female patients, he finally sucumbed to the lure of the market place. When manufacturers of carpet sweepers, washing machines and other appliances used by women began calling their products "Women's Friend," Pengelly bestowed on his preparation a name as mysterious as its secret ingredients - Zoa-Phora.

In 1885 three prominent Kalamazooans took over management of the Zoa-Phora Medicine Company from Pengelly. Latham Hull, president of the First National Bank also became president of Zoa-Phora; Samuel A. Gibson, superintendent of the Kalamazoo Paper Company, became vice-president; and druggist Howard G. Colman, secretary and treasurer.

Pengelly, however, remained actively involved in the company's operations and especially lent his good name to its vigorous promotional efforts. With each bottle of Zoa-Phora came Pengelly's prize pamphlet, a treatise on female complaints and sex guide, wrapped, of course, in plain brown paper.

Huge Zoa-Phora newspaper displays, "Good News for Women" and "Saved From Insanity," jostled similar Lydia Pinkham advertisements. One 1895 advertisement announced, "What Zoa-Phora won't do for womanhood no medicine will." Another labeled Zoa-Phora "Women's Friend" and offered deliverance from "the slough of despondence and a sickness worse than death." Effective for women of any age, the nostrum proffered "a steady hand to guide the frail and sickly girl to and through the trying period that opens to her the untraveled paths of womanhood." It then made "the hour of maternity almost free from pain and agony" and was the "friend and mainstay" of women passing "from the period of motherhood to the last period of life." The nostrum sold for a dollar in bottles curiously resembling pint whiskey flasks.

Mary Pengelly, wife of the discoverer of Zoa-Phora, was active in the Women's Christian Temperance Union (WCTU); so active, in fact, that the local unit was named in her honor. In June 1902, matronly teetotalers from across Michigan descended upon the Celery City for the annual state WCTU convention. On the page of the *Kalamazoo Gazette* devoted to the last session of this gathering of prohibitionists, myopic Dr. and Mrs. Pengelly innocently peered from the center of a huge advertisement headed "W.C.T.U. Members and Prominent Kalamazoo Ladies Praise Zoa-Phora." Until the company folded in 1910, Victorian sufferers and suffragettes alike found their lives "buoyed up" by Zoa-Phora.

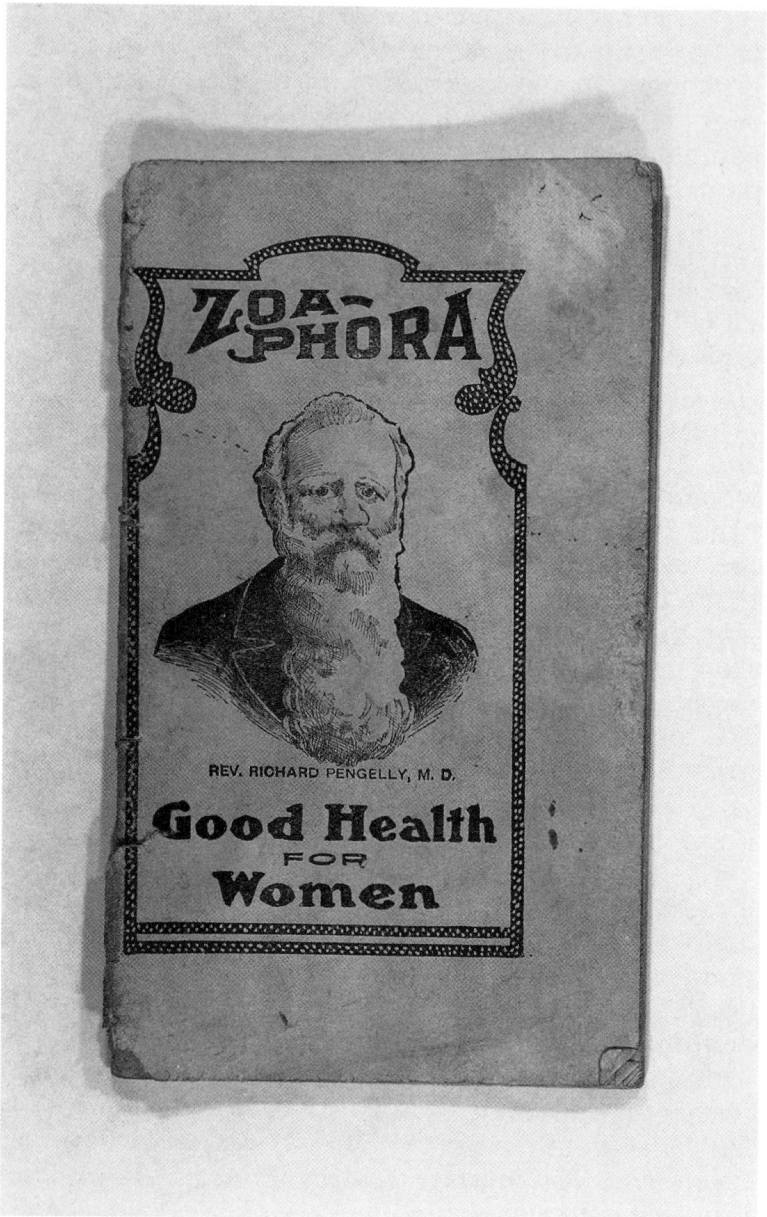

The Rev., Dr., Pengelly's Sex Guide featured his visage on the cover.

Other local manufacturers created similar cures for rheumatism. D.D. Brown, a South Burdick Street druggist, offered his Rheumatic Elixir. Eccentric old Henry W. Rood, who claimed to have learned a wonderful formula from Indian medicine men out west, compounded the alliterative"Rood's Rheumatism Remedy." And Burdick Street druggists, Frederick Glass and son, created "Forest Oil." The classical image evoked by the Forest Oil logo, a youth gaining wisdom at the feet of an ancient chemist was somewhat marred by its motto:

> Our stock is fresh
> Our drugs are pure
> Forest Oil will cure you sure.

Not all patent medicines needed to be imbibed orally. The label of Dr. E. Fenton's "Great Catarrh Annihilater," for example, directed sufferers: "Turn out in the palm of the hand one tablespoonful. Snuff the liquid up the nostrils as hard and as high as you can until the liquid passes to the throat, no harm can arise. Use two or three times in five minutes and you will find the pain gone." Enos Fenton, who manufactured this remarkable remedy for "catarrh, colds in the head, nervous headache, neuralgia, sore eyes, and loss of smell and taste," appeared in the 1873 *Kalamazoo City Directory* as a clerk. By 1876 he had become a doctor, as well as a practical druggist and dealer in "pure drugs, chemicals, patent medicines, fancy goods, toilet articles, and perfume." The only testimony to the effectiveness of the Great Catarrh Annihilator is the fact that Fenton failed to appear at all in the next city directory.

Kalamazoo sufferers also had access to many mysterious cures beyond the realm of patent medicines. In 1869, the *Kalamazoo City Directory* announced that Dr. James Moliere, "Natural Healer

Victorians enjoyed celery spiced concoctions at drug stores such as Van Ostrands in Allegan (1898).

and Magnetic Physician," and Madame Florence Moliere, "the Medical and Business Clairvoyant," had permanently located at the Magnetic Infirmary in the Masonic Building on Main Street. Dr. Moliere based his treatments on the popular belief that a magnetic or electrical charge contained in the human body could become imbalanced and affect one's health. The Molieres ran a simple husband and wife operation: Madame Moliere clairvoyantly delineated the disease without questioning the patient, and the doctor applied the remedies, including "hot air, vapor, electric, and chemical baths." The Molieres also failed to appear in the next city directory.

But in 1870, Kalamazooans opened their newspapers to learn of "The Great Spiritual Remedy" - Mrs. Spence's Positive and Negative Powders. "Men, women and children," they read, "find them a silent but sure success" - the positive powders, it seems, cured complaints ranging from neuralgia and diarrhea to worms, fits, catarrh and St. Vitus dance - the negatives were good for paralysis, deafness, typhoid fever and nervous prostration - for chills and fevers a dose of both positive and negative was indicated.

In 1870, also, Kalamazooans discovered that Dr. H. Slade, clairvoyant, and J. Simmons, formerly of Jackson, had located in Kalamazoo. Slade's clairvoyant abilities allowed him to successfully prescribe for patients at a distance by receiving a lock of hair with name and age" - and, of course, a $2 deposit. Slade later made his mark by his discovery that he possessed the ability to communicate with the hereafter via "spirit slate writing" - also for a fee.

Professor R.J. Lyons, who in 1876 was available for consultation on the twentieth and twenty-first of each month at his room in the Burdick House, offered similar convenience. He "discerned diseases by the eye," and advertisements specified,

"He asks no questions, neither does he require invalids to explain their symptoms." Lyons, a naturopathist, prescribed only "roots, barks, leaves, and seeds" and specialized in "diseases of women," whom he encouraged to "come in as early as possible."

Another naturopathic physician, Dr. Redner, announced in 1878 that he had hung out his shingle at 20 Portage Street. His list of area testimonials included an Oshtemo resident cured of a twelve-year-long liver complaint, who "would not be placed back where he was for his whole farm" and a sixteen-year victim of catarrh of the bladder, stomach and bowels, who after a week's treatment, "would not be placed back where he was for the best farm in the state of Michigan." That evidently was Dr. Redner's fee - a cure for a farm.

Dr. Sarah E. Morrill, author of *Treatise of Practical Instructions in the Medical and Surgical Uses of Electricity* (1882) developed a rather simple procedure for diagnosis. Patients sat in a chair, their feet immersed in cold water, while she ran a wand discharging electricity up and down their spine. Where they felt the current "shoot through to the front of the body" was obviously the ailing part. Treatment consisted of further electrical jolts to the afflicted organs.

Medicinal baths were also a popular treatment in the Celery City. In 1895 the newly organized Hygeia Sanitarium appropriately located on Asylum Avenue, now Oakland Drive, advertised "baths of every description, electricity in every form, massage, Swedish movements, mechanical movements, and pneumatic and vacuum treatments as required." It staggers the imagination to ponder what they were doing with air pressure and vacuum treatments then.

The Kalamazoo Treatment Rooms at 115 East South Street featured fomentations, electric bath, salt

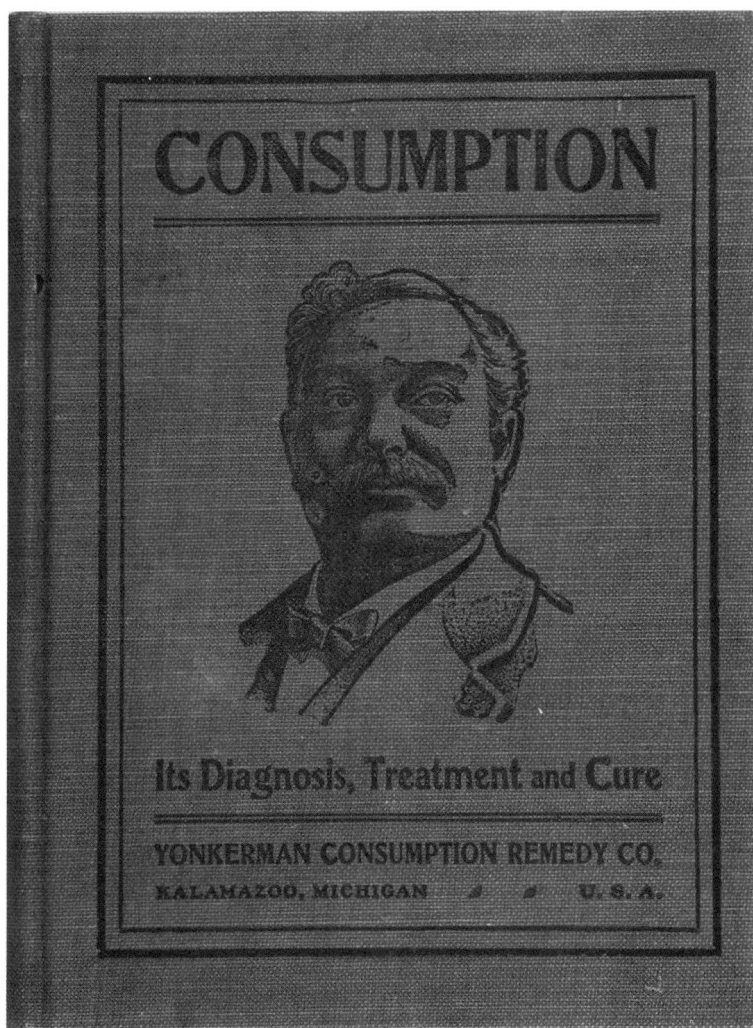

CONSUMPTION

Its Diagnosis, Treatment and Cure

YONKERMAN CONSUMPTION REMEDY CO.

KALAMAZOO, MICHIGAN   U. S. A.

Dr. Dirk Yonkerman, a veterinarian, presented copies of his treatise on tuberculosis with bottles of his bogus cure.

glow and massage for $1.00. They also offered board and room at moderate prices, presumbly for those not able to walk away after the treatments. And the turn of the century, suffers from all forms rheumatism, lumbago, paralysis and bowel, stomach and nerve troubles could also visit Bowditch B. Frazee at his East Main Street baths. There they might choose from steam, electrical, saline, medicated, shower and needle, sulphur, tonic, friction, hydropath, pack, sitz, herb and antiseptic baths.

Medical chicanery continued to thrive during the first decade of the twentieth century, though Progressives began to advocate laws to curb it. Spurred by the rise of factories such as the Kalamazoo Stove Company and the many paper mills that made it America's largest paper producer, the city grew in population by 62 percent. Celery entrepreneur Dunkley attributed that population growth to an increase in the birthrate brought about through the use of his aphrodisiac, Celerytone. "Kalamazoo is the home of celery," Dunklety boasted, "and is peopled with healthy, sturdy men and beautiful women; they all drink Celerytone."

Panaceas abounded throughout the decade. In 1902, from her Alamo Avenue residence, Mrs. C.H. Stimpson offered cures for "a bearing-down sensation, sense of impending evils, pain in the back or back of head or bowels, creeping feelings up the spine, sick headache, dark rings under the eyes, and tears shed easily." Sufferers need only take a few doses of her Opaline suppositories, whose principal ingredients Food and Drug Administration analysts later found to be borax, alum and opium.

John VerWest manufactured Odell's Wonderful Oil, that could either be applied like liniment or drunk, to cure "rheumatism, neuralgia, kidney trouble, lame back, toothache, diarrhea, cramps, cuts, burns, and aches of all kinds." It was also, according to his 1904 advertisement, a fine thing for horses in case of stomach ache or spavin.

Balding Kalamazooans of the period might choose between a variety of hair-growing treatments ranging from "Harrison's Hair Hastener," developed by a Burdick Street barber, druggist William McDonald's "Quinine Hair Tonic" or "Jackson's Influx Hair Grower and Medicated Soap" which was guaranteed "to grow hair on the baldest head without reference to cause of baldness or time bald." For those with too much hair, particularly women with superfluous hair on the face, neck or arms, E.M. Kennedy dispensed vials of "Kill-All-Hair" treatment at his drugstore at 104 West Main Street.

Madame Cook, at her hair dressing establishment located on East Main Street over Witwer's Bakery, offered "Skin Food" as a remedy for tan, freckles, sunburn and moth patches the yellow pigmented spots now known as chloasma. And madam A.L. Hobbs on South Burdick Street supplied tonics guaranteed as a "skin bleacher" that cured and eradicated permanently brown spots, wrinkles, freckles, pimples, and those stubborn moth patches. For the skeptics, Madam Hobbs kept on hand a supply of patients who had applied her remedy to only one side of their faces.

While most of those medical confidence games, did little good for the ill, they merely extracted money without permanently damaging the body. Some, however, were downright dangerous. In 1903, the Kalamazoo Institute of Natural Therapeutics promised cures for consumption, catarrh, hay fever, asthma, deafness, rheumatism and blood poison and guaranteed a cure in every case of face eruptions. The miraculous treatment was the X-ray, "whose static breezes stop all pain and kill the germs." During an era when pioneer radiologists known as the martyrs inadvertently gave themselves radium poisoning,

149

quacks were deliberately exposing their patients' faces and other body parts to long jolts of the X-ray.

Kalamazoo's grandest medical fraud, however, was that perpetrated by the Yonkerman Consumption Remedy Company. It operated from somewhere within the huge old mansard style building located on the corner of Rose and Water streets. Originally the Lawrence and Chapin Iron Works, later the Interurban Station and Vermeulen's Furniture Store and recently refurbished to its original architectural splendor, the structure at that time housed the Shakespeare Manufacturing Company. William Shakespeare, Jr., inventor of the "wonderreel" and other popular fishing tackle, had registered the brand name "Tuberculozyne" in 1905. He served as secretary-treasurer when the company was founded, but soon dropped behind the scenes to become a silent partner.

Bottles of Tuberculozyne displayed the honest-looking face and signature of the front man, Dr. Derk P. Yonkerman, a registered veterinarian. Yonkerman purportedly discovered his treatment through mysterious experimentation on a herd of condemned tubercular cattle. After treatment and postmortem examination, surgeons "were astounded to find the supposed tubercular organs completely healed." Dr. Yonkerman was then "persuaded" to permit his treatment on humans.

It was a classic patent medicine scam. Nationally circulated advertisements proclaimed Tuberculozyne "the only known remedy for consumption." Respondents received a booklet filled with testimonials and case histories implying a connection between tuberculosis and La Grippe, croup, catarrh and night sweats. A mail carrier from Georgia claimed he "would have been a dead man if it had not been for your Tuberculozyne." A thirty-four-year-old housewife from Arkansas said that she too "would have been dead if it had not been for your medicine," but instead had "been picking cotton all fall." The mother of a six-year-old sufferer wrote that after twenty doctors had failed, ten treatments of Tuberculozyne made the child "the perfect picture of health." The nostrum, on analysis, proved to be chiefly a mixture of glycerine, water, burnt sugar and a dash of essential oil of almonds for flavor. Yonkerman charged ten dollars for a bottle containing five cents worth of ingredients.

Gullible sufferers who ordered the initial bottle were hounded to continue treatment. Correspondence sent out under Yonkerman's letterhead, featuring a view of the massive Mansard building he claimed as headquarters, quoted additional heart-wrenching testimonials and warned of the "sad results of stopping too soon - a fatal mistake. Better to take a whole month's treatment more than is needed than to stop a week or day too soon." The year following the adoption of the Pure Food and Drug Act of 1906, Yonkerman toned down his advertising in America and established a branch office in London, England, where drug advertising was not yet regulated. Eventually, however, even the Australian government forbade the importation of Tuberculozyne, and in 1916, after more than a decade of bilking the sick, the Yonkerman Remedy Company closed shop. Shakespeare continued to manufacture his world-renowned fishing tackle; and Yonkerman returned to his "veterinary surgeon" practice.

The Pure Food and Drug Act cut the ground out from under most medical frauds. It did not prohibit false advertising entirely, but it enforced truthful advertising of effects and the listing of contents. Without the aid of extravagant advertising, and with alcohol and narcotic ingredients exposed on the label, patent medicines lost much of their glamour. Yet, many survived, albeit with reduced strengths and claims. As late as 1927, the Gilbert Goiter Remedy

Company announced its incorporation in Kalamazoo.

Today, the medical foibles of the Celery City seem humorous. Nevertheless, this colorful chicanery was typical of the situation in hundreds of other American towns and cities. Imaginative, if unscrupulous, entrepreneurs catered to needs left unfilled by traditional medicine, powerless in the face of many now curable afflictions. Despite flim-flam promotion and Victorian gullibility, alcohol and narcotic nostrums must have dulled much genuine pain. Furthermore, considering the recognized value of psychosomatic suggestion, patent medicines undoubtedly brought some curative relief. And while comparison of archaic and current technology proves amusing, it will be interesting to witness twenty-first century evaluations of the medical vogues of the present.

They Had Sawdust In Their Hair & Ink In Their Veins: Michigan's Literary Lumberjacks

The boys were whooping it up at the Seney Bar. Jammed with a typical Saturday night crowd, that tough lumberjack lair was no place for a lady - or for a man who couldn't drink his liquor straight and give or take a good punch to the jaw. Drawn by the ruddy glow of the bar's window and the muffled roar of merriment within, new customers crunched through the snow. Each time the door swung open a babel of gruff laughter, curses, boastful storytelling and calls for more drinks blasted the crisp night air.

To the rear of the smoke-filled room at a table alone sat a grizzled old character with his face to the wall. He wore the familiar uniform of a lumberjack, a plaid Mackinaw hat, matching heavy wool pants tucked into rolled-over sock tops, a pair of broad red suspenders and a faded blue flannel shirt open at the throat to reveal long underwear beneath. Nearby, against the wall, leaned a bright-bladed double bitted ax. The old man's huge slumped shoulders, bull neck and enormous forearms resting against the table warned of brute strength.

He stared at the wall, lost in reverie, oblivious to the boisterous crowd, a nearby arm wrestling match and two French Canadians arguing over who was the best man in the woods. Suddenly he reached out for a shot glass, tossed its contents to the back of his throat, slowly stood up, grabbed his ax just below the blade and, clomping one worn leather boot on a chair, climbed atop the table. As he turned to face the crowd, knees bent slightly, head thrust forward, glowering, the room quieted, until save for one loud mouth in a far corner, everyone had turned to stare at the old lumberjack. And then when the final patron ceased his haranguing, the old man bellowed in a gravelly voice, "You know I've heard a lot of cheap talk tonight and now its my turn. I'm gonna tell you about the 1870s and 1880s, my heyday, when pine was king in Michigan. When thousands of men like myself made our living in the woods. Folks called us lumberjacks, they called us shanty boys, they called us river men - some even called us river hogs - but they better have laughed when they did! Frankly I never cared what they called me - just so long as when cookee beat that gut hammer he was calling me to supper!" The old man cackled a deep throaty laugh echoed by a half dozen others in the crowd, and then he continued.

"I've logged the Tittabawassee, the Tahquamenon, the Muskegon and the Grand. I've rode cork pine down the Menominee, the Chippewa, the Pentwater and the Pere Marquette. My caulked boots have scarred the wooden sidewalks of Newberry, Red Keg, Ludington, Saginaw and most every other lumber town in these two peninsulas. And when I wasn't in the swamps wrestling wood or on the white water burling logs, I drank enough red eye to float a wanigan."

"I was one of the red sash brigade that finished axing our way across the state of Maine in the 1840s. Then we heard about Michigan. What we heard didn't nearly measure up to what we saw when we got here. Why, there were trees so big that three men together couldn't get their arms around them. They reached 150 feet into the air, straight as an arrow. That virgin timber land lay as far as you could see in all directions. Those pines blanketed the Saginaw River Valley, the Thumb, they stretched from the Kalamazoo all the way to the Straits of Mackinac and

This paintings by Edith Browning Brand illustrated Puddefoot and Rankin's 1903 *Hewers of Wood*.

across the whole U.P."

"Oh, sure there was maple, walnut, cherry and oak aplenty too, but we didn't much care for hardwood. We wanted pine - white pine in particular - green gold we called it - cork pine so light it floated like a cork in the water."

"Let me tell you, it was hard work in the lumber camps and dangerous too. More than one shanty boy lost his life to a widow-maker, as we called a big old dead branch ready to fall. We worked from dawn to dusk - making daylight in the swamp - and when cookee blew his big tin gabriel or pounded the triangle you can bet we raced for the cookhouse - and the devil take the hindmost. And when we hit our bunks at night it took more than a few bites from the big grayback bed bugs that infested the place to keep us awake."

"I guess at one time or another I've done just about everything there was to be done in the lumber camps. Everything but cook that is - I can't cook worth beans - and I'm here to tell you that a lumber camp cook that didn't cook good and lots of it - wasn't long for the world around those hungry jacks."

"I was a timber cruiser for a while. Took a map and a compass and tramped the wilderness for weeks looking for a prime stand located near a stream. When I found one I made a beeline for the nearest government land office to stake a claim. Not that that always mattered. I've worked for more than one boss who cut a round forty - that is, he bought forty acres, then cut all the trees as far as you could see around it."

The old man cackled again at his joke, took in a big gulp of air, and began again.

"I've worked as a road monkey, slashing a tote road into the site. I've worked as a tote teamster, hauling in supplies and equipment. I've worked as a wood butcher, nailing together the primitive shanties we lived in - and let me tell you - more than one's the winter morning I woke up with snow drifted through the cracks in the wall right across my bunk."

"We never worried much about cold in the daytime though - we were too damn busy to notice it."

"Believe me I've spent many a long winter in the woods as a shanty boy, felling trees with my doubled bitted ax - Michigan pattern - on the business end of a crosscut saw bucking trees into 16 foot lengths, skidding logs to the cross haul with oxen - loading huge bobsled loads with my cant hook."

"Once I worked a sprinkler at night, icing the trail for easy sledding. Once, when I was down on my luck, I signed on as a chickadee - my humble task being to keep the logging trails free of road apples."

"But when spring came, and the ice and snow melted and the streams rose to drive pitch, I pulled on my caulked boots and swapped my ax for a peavy. I became a river hog and when they turned those mountains of logs loose at the rollway I rode them down stream, looking for logs stranded in the back water, and breaking up log jams along the way. Once I remember I came around a bend in the Tittabawassee and there was a dirty, low down timber pirate cutting off the end of a log marked with our initials and preparing to pound on his own brand. I bet he won't be doing that again real soon!"

"Well, anyway, when we got to the sorting booms up stream from the sawmills at Saginaw, Muskegon, Menominee or wherever we were, our job was done. We collected our hard earned pay - $100 or so for a long winter's work. You can bet we were right ready to spend a little too - sometimes all of it - for a good time. The name of the game was booze, bawds and battle - and those lumber towns stood more than ready to oblige us."

A squad of river hogs posed for the camera below the lower dam on the Menominee River in 1887.

"Once I battled a big Swede from Camp 16 for over two hours just to prove who was cock of the walk. I hit him and he hit me! I knocked him down and he knocked me down, and so it went - all day long it seemed - finally I hit him so hard he couldn't get back up - you know what I done then? I reached out my hand, pulled him to his feet and we went and had a drink together."

The memory of that prodigious battle and the effects of his rapid fire monologue caused the old shanty boy to go into a paroxysm of coughing. Deep rumbling hacks from the bottom of his lungs wracked his body. The barroom waited, watching spellbound. Would the old man master his attack and continue? They knew, full well, he had more to say.

The truth of the matter was that the old lumberjack's performance had become a standard Saturday night spectacle - awaited and appreciated by the regulars. Nor was the Seney Bar the only watering hole where colorful old lumberjacks relived the glory days of their youth. During the first decades of the twentieth century as sawmills buzzed and whined their way through the last of the virgin white pine and other forest giants that once blanketed the peninsulas, in Muskegon and Saginaw, Ludington and Cadillac, Menominee and Newberry and a hundred other places that once echoed with brawling river hogs, old timers told stories of how it used to be, spun Paul Bunyan yarns and sang ballads of shanty boys and log jams. While most of that rich body of oral tradition and folklore followed the tellers to the grave, unrecorded, fortunately, a variety of those who participated in the felling of the pine swapped ax and peavey for the pen and published their experiences in autobiographies, novels, short stories and poems. The efforts of those scribbling shanty boys survive as a literary legacy well worth the reading.

A number of lumbermen chose the traditional

method of autobiography to record their experiences. Some of those books circulated widely while other privately-printed thin volumes remain little known sources of lumberjack lore. Sixteen-year-old Charles Blakeman, for example, left his family homestead in Allegan County's Otsego Township in 1878 to become a shanty boy in the pine forests near Stanton. The following year he secured a job felling trees in the Cadillac area. Half a century later he privately printed a little volume of reminiscences, *Report of a Truant* (Grand Rapids, 1928). An incident he experienced following a season working as a river hog reveals that the lumberjack sport of street brawling was not necessarily fun or fair:

> After several months of steady, long, hard days of driving they were in a saloon town and were allowed time to "celebrate." A quarrel attracted Charles' attention. A man too drunk to make any considerable defense was being trampled by another drunken brute named Bishop. The extreme unfairness of it caused Charles to ignore reason or caution, and he jolted the bully away from his victim, only to go down himself at the finish, after having inflicted a painful bruise on Bishop's face. Not willing to beat up Charles and let him off with that, he drew a quart bottle from his pocket. It was nearly full of whisky, adding enough weight so it was a very deadly weapon. He raised it full arm's length, giving it swing enough to crush a skull. But at that moment his arm was seized by a powerful fellow who was able to subdue him.

Lumberjack literature abounds with vivid descriptions of epic fights. But shanty boys and river hogs claimed no monopoly on the manly art of fisticuffs. Other hard working laborers such as railroad workers apparently shared a similar bellicose nature. Robert Dollar, a Scottish immigrant who would eventually become a multimillionaire via lumbering and shipping, had shifted his operations from Canada to the Upper Peninsula of Michigan in 1882. As recorded in the first volume of his *Memoirs* published in 1918, he established a sawmill in Luce County at a site named in his honor, Dollarville, and then took to the wilderness to locate prime stands of timber. On one such foray he experienced a gandy dancers' donnybrook:

With a man to help me I went to the end of the railroad and camped in a house kept by a Mr. O'Brien and his wife. They had gotten a barrel of whiskey to celebrate Christmas and New Year's and it was about empty, but they were to have a last blow-out that night. When I went into the kitchen on my arrival, Mrs. O'Brien was busy grating blue stone (blue vitriol or copper sulphate, used as a dye, germicide and insecticide) and putting it into the whiskey barrel. I asked her what in the world she was doing, and she told me they had all made up their minds to have a big last drunk that night, and as she had found there was not enough whiskey she knew there would be the dickens to pay, and the only thing she had to make it out of was pepper and bluestone, with water and what little whiskey was left in the bottom of the barrel.

I said we had better go and tent out as we had all the outfit with us, and I did not want to be in a place like that, but she said it was a terrible, cold night and on no account to leave as we could go into a lower bunk in the corner and no harm would come to us. So with her assurance we remained. The men, about twenty-five of them, came in at dark and had supper. They were a very quiet looking lot of fellows, mostly Irishmen. After supper they started drinking. My man and myself went to bed with the ground for the bottom of our berth where there were several roots and small stumps that made it anything but level or soft. However, we spread out our blankets and as we were tired we were soon asleep. About midnight we were awakened by a terrible row. The lamp was knocked out and the big stove overturned and smashed to pieces, and the contents went flying all over the shanty setting it on fire in many places. The men all made a rush for the door and got out into the snow. As it was many degrees below zero and we were in our bare feet we were in a bad way. The drunkest ones came out into the snow to get more room to finish their fight, and the more sober ones to throw snow and water on the burning shanty. So we got to work and assisted in saving the building. Rolling in the snow had the effect of putting an end to the fight, and quiet was restored.

We had breakfast and were glad to get ready for our departure, having seen enough of the results of Mrs. O'Brien's blue-stone whiskey combination. While we were packing up our provisions I could not find the flour we had. I asked the landlady if she had seen it, and she said "Sure enough I saw it; I got short and have used it all up!" So we were forced to return that night again, but supplies had arrived that day so we replaced our flour and went on our way rejoicing to sleep in the snow which we preferred to O'Brien's hostelry.

Timber cruisers like Dollar initiated the cycle of the forest harvest. Tramping the wilderness while prospecting for prime stands, they sometimes discovered timber bonanzas. Michigan's lumber industry had barely left its cradle days when John

Driving a six ox team took skill.

Ball, a 41-year-old immigrant from New Hampshire, caught the Michigan land fever in 1836 and set up headquarters in the frontier boom town of Grand Rapids. From there he conducted land looking and timber cruising forays west through Kent, Ottawa and Allegan counties. In his posthumous *Autobiography* published by his daughters in 1925, Ball recorded some early timber cruising adventures in the Grand River Valley wilderness. During one wintry exploration to Ottawa County, Ball discovered a 2,500 acre tract of virgin white pine and a stand of enormous white oak trees, one of which was seven feet in diameter. Although he succeeded in entering the entire tract at the federal land office in Ionia at the going price for government land - $1.25 an acre - the subsequent Panic of 1837 sent prices crashing on the Michigan frontier and elsewhere and he failed to profit from his lucky find. When the worst effects of the depression subsided "Honest" John Ball's knowledge of the wilderness learned during his timber cruising stood him in good stead and he ultimately made a fortune from his land dealings.

Isaac Stephenson, another skilled timber cruiser who would forge a fortune out of the frontier - in his case the Upper Peninsula - also recorded his lumbering experiences in an autobiography, *Recollections of a Long Life* (Chicago, 1915). The Upper Peninsula lumber industry was also in its infancy in 1846 when the 17-year-old Stephenson arrived at a logging camp located about 25 miles up the Escanaba River. Stephenson had worked in the woods since he was eleven in his native New Brunswick and Maine and during that first Michigan winter he plied his skill in driving a six ox team, hauling out 150 forest giants as long as 107 feet, highly valued as ship's masts. He penned descriptions of life in the Escanaba lumber camps at that early period:

We were up for breakfast at five o'clock and off to work before daylight and so did not return until dark... The rations upon which we thrived were, to say the least meager, and there was not enough variety to tempt even a normal appetite. As there were no farms in the vicinity to rely upon, the supply of vegetables was small. We were rarely able to obtain any at all. For five and one half months during one winter we did not see a vegetable and were given fresh meat only once. Camp fare consisted of the inevitable pork and beans, bread and tea which we sweetened with Porto Rico molasses in lieu of sugar. Occasionally we had a little butter and dried apples but so infrequently that they seemed a luxury beyond the conception of even the lumber men of the present day who have varied camp supply lists to draw upon for sustenance.

For breakfast and supper the beverage was tea, for dinner, only water. Sometimes when I was detained, arriving late at the mess table, I found the water which had been poured into my tin cup frozen and had to break the ice to drink... Sunday, as in the East also, was a day of rest, the kind of rest that takes the form of a change of occupation. The men in charge of the camps made axe handles, filed saws and ground axes. Despite all the apparent hardships, the long hours, the hazardous nature of the work, and the lack of luxuries we did well enough. Our work was such that we needed no special stimulus to whet our appetites. We made the most of our unvarying fare and ate with a zest that comes only of long days of work in the open, the keen, crisp air of the winter and the tang of the pine forests.

John Emmett Nelligan, another New Brunswick native who immigrated to the Upper Great Lakes pine lands in 1871, spent the next half century working as a timber cruiser, woods-foreman, river boss and contractor. He published his recollections in 1929 as *The Life of a Lumberman*. The tough Irish lumberjack described how food and camp life had evolved from Stephenson's era to the heyday of Upper Peninsula logging during the last quarter of the 19th century:

The daily routine of life in a lumber camp began long before the break of day. At about four o'clock in the morning the chore boy, awakened by an alarm clock or, more often, by that sixth sense which warns a man that the designated hour of awakening is at hand, would crawl from his cozy nest of warm blankets into the chill early morning atmosphere and start the fires - one in the cook's camp, one in the men's camp, and a third in the camp office, where the foreman and the scaler and perhaps one or two others slept. When a good healthy blaze was roaring in each of the three stoves and waves of warmth were attacking the blanket of cold which lay over the camp like a pall, the chore boy would go into the men's camp and shake the teamsters into wakefulness, being careful not to disturb the sleep of the other men. The chore boy's popularity among the jacks depended largely upon his discretion in this matter. The teamsters would sleepily and noiselessly arise, pull on their outer garments, and depart for the barns, where they fed, cleaned and harnessed their horses in preparation for the day's work. This done, they returned to the camp, dressed their feet fully, washed for breakfast and, perhaps, took a chew of plug tobacco as an appetizer.

By the time the teamsters were ready for breakfast, the camp reveille, blown on a big tin horn, roused the rest of the camp at about 4:35 A.M., and the jacks had rolled out of their blankets, pulled on the

An odoriferous turn of the century lumber camp bunkhouse.

clothes they had taken off the night before - few enough, in truth - taken their heavy socks from the drying racks, donned them and were washing for breakfast.

At 4:50 or 5:00 A.M. the "gaberal" would blow the breakfast horn as a signal to the jacks to "come and get it." There would be a rush for the long tables in the cook shanty and a pitched battle would ensue between the lumberjacks and the marvelous products of the cook's culinary efforts, with the jacks invariably the victors. Breakfast in a lumber camp was no such light meal as the morning fruit, cereal, and coffee tidbits eaten by modern business men. It was as large and important a meal as any other and the bill of fare could read more like a dinner than a breakfast to the average person of today. Flapjacks or pancakes, sometimes of buck wheat, fried as only a lumber camp cook can fry them, stacked in great piles along the oil cloth covered tables, were favorite items of fare among the jacks. But there might be baked beans, or fried meat, hash potatoes, or any other dish which could be prepared from the extensive larder. All this washed down with great draughts of coffee, coffee with such fragrance that one's nose crinkles with remembrance at the thought of it. And there were tasty cookies and cakes.

The men were never given an opportunity to complain about the bill of fare in our camps, nor in any other camps for that matter. Lumberjacks were always fed well. They demanded it and it paid the camp operators to feed them well. The better they were fed, the better work they did.

Breakfast over, the men pulled on their outer working clothes and departed for their various posts. Most of them wore wool caps, heavy flannel shirts, Mackinaw cloth jackets and pants, heavy German socks and low rubbers. This was the warmest, most comfortable, and most efficient costume for woods work. When the scene of the cutting wasn't too far from the camp, the men returned to the cook shanty for their midday meal, but when it was some distance away, the "flaggin's" were carried to them on a large sled by the chore boys. Great, thick sandwiches, large cans full of hot food from which the jacks filled their tin plates, and great, steaming cans of hot tea satisfied the midday hunger.

Back to work they went and labored until after dark. Conditions are somewhat changed now, but in those days there was no eight hour day and while there was day-light the work went on. Then they would straggle into camp and eat their evening meal with appetites such as only tired and hungry men can develop. The teamsters put away and cared for their horses before eating. After supper the jacks would gather around the great red-hot stove in the bunkhouse, pull off their wet, stinking socks and hang them on the drying racks around and above the stove, where they steamed away and emitted an indescribably atrocious odor which permeated the bunkhouse atmosphere.

George A. Corrigan, another lumberman who boasted lineage from the land of leprechauns, spent 25 years in the woods of Ashland and Iron counties, Wisconsin and Gogebic County, Michigan, beginning in 1912. His colorful recollections published in 1976 as *Calked Boots and Cant Hooks* offer valuable insight on the preservation of foods in the lumber camp:

Since there was no refrigeration, storage of fresh foodstuffs was a major undertaking. Sometimes oleomargarine or lard was kept in a spring or creek but in the very early days, no attempt was made to keep butter. Fresh meat was part of the diet in summer, but camps did serve venison or moose in the fall in areas where there was a surplus of those animals. In the winter the companies were able to tote in frozen meat of all kinds.

In the summer the cooks used screen houses to keep what meat they could receive. A screen house is a building with a rectangular roof to keep the sun from shining too directly on it, built about four feet off the ground on blocks. The walls were built of boards about three feet up, then about four feet of screen wire all around to keep out flies and other insects. The building had long eaves so the sun's rays couldn't get in and the air circulating through the screened sides would keep the meat hanging on hooks dry, with very little spoilage, especially of smoked meats. This method worked quite well (although, of course, you could not expect to keep meat over long periods of time) and was the storage method in general use until about 1940 when some camps began to have ice boxes or refrigeration.

Root houses, excavations in the side of a hill, supported by double tiers of logs with solid door, located as near the kitchen as possible, were used for storing potatoes, turnips and other root vegetables for use in the fall and winter months.

One final autobiographical account of Michigan lumbering, and the only such first person account to be written by a woman, should be considered. In 1951 Julie Anderson published *I Married A Logger*, a fascinating account of her and her husband Howard's experiences in running a lumber camp near Wakefield during the Depression era. Monday meant wash day for most Americans, but as Anderson observed, that weekly task fell to the lumberjacks on Sunday:

The jacks appeared at the back of the bunk- house
to prepare for their Sunday "boiling-up." From
the office window, Howard and I watched them
while we waited for breakfast bell. Under the big
black kettle that hung on a pole wired between
two sturdy maples, the jacks kindled a roaring fire.
They pumped pail after pail of water to fill the
kettle. After breakfast, when the steam began to
rise above the rim of the kettle, each jack waited
for his turn to scoop out bucketfuls of hot wash
water into a tub on the bench nearby.
Using a tin can punched full of holes at one end
and nailed to a long stick, the jacks soused their
underwear and socks around in the steaming
sudsy water until they became the desired shade of
gray. With quick twists the jacks wrung the
steaming sudsy water out of their things and rinsed
them in a tub of clear water. They squeezed out
the rinse water and secured the clothes to a line
strung between saplings, or they hung them on
broken branches of trees.
There the clothes remained until they dried. Some
hung limp from the line, and other twisted and
clung to the trees. Frozen stiff in winter or flopping
crazily in the spring breezes, these assorted shirts,
holey socks, and tattered or patched underwear
made a queer sight. By noon time on Sunday all
who had washing to do, and the ambition to do it,
had taken their turn at tending the fire, carrying
water, and sousing their clothes in sudsy water.

Not all literary lumberjacks wrote autobiographies. Some chose the medium of fiction to
record their observations. John W. Fitzmaurice, a run-
down newspaper editor who visited over 400 lumber
camps in northern Michigan and Wisconsin in the

171

1880s, wrote the first book-length fiction about Michigan logging, *The Shanty Boy; or Life in a Lumber Camp* (Cheboygan, 1889). The volume contains a fascinating collection of anecdotes, poetry and stories recited at the "deacon's seat" gathered during Fitzmaurice's travels selling hospital tickets, an early form of medical insurance, to the shanty boys. Typical of his style and use of genuine lumberjack slang is Fitzmaurice's description of a trick played on a sky-pilot, as itinerant missionaries who visited lumber camps were termed:

> One well meaning man, with lots of zeal but not according to knowledge, visited a certain Michigan camp, which shall in this telling, be nameless. He gave the men an after supper address in the bunk camp, and told them how dirty they were, and how foul and polluted their habits and language were, and kept that strain up for half an hour, concluding by telling them he was "engaged in the Lord's work," and if they liked to take up a little collection and give it to him, the next morning before leaving camp, he would be much obliged.
> This was done by one of the "toughs" of the camp, and the "collection" was taken before the men went to bed. He gathered the "collection" in a pill box, and all hands contributed liberally to fill it with personal "live stock." The old gentleman was up bright and early and was at the breakfast table, bent over, busy eating with his neck very much exposed, when the "collector" in passing him emptied the contents of the pill box down the back of his neck, and quietly passed on to his seat at the table. It was a beastly trick I admit, but such is life in camp, and frequently very much "lice-ence" is permitted, when you don't happen to strike it just right. The wonder is that they didn't "put him up."

River hogs faced many dangers such as breaking log jams.

Fitzmaurice's observation that in all his travels he had "yet to hear of or see one man who has expressed any benefit from the visit of the camp missionary" did little to prevent numerous sky-pilots from carrying their various brands of religion to the "Godless lumber camps." And as might be expected, some of them wrote books about their experiences. William G. Puddefoot, a Tecumseh shoemaker, caught the Congregationalist spirit in 1879 and left his last and hammer to carry the word to the pine lands, preaching at Gaylord, White Cloud, Rockford, Traverse City, Sugar Island and across the Upper Peninsula. He wrote two autobiographical accounts in part detailing his Michigan adventures and in 1903 collaborated with Isaac Ogden Rankin to pen a novel *Hewers of Wood: A Story of the Michigan Pine Forests.* Much of the plot is set at Camp Number 10 on the Shiawassee River. The book provides a description of river men:

> These men were the cavaliers of the lumber business. They attired themselves in a red Mackinaw shirt, which bade defiance to rain or snow, French kip boots, which cost eighteen dollars a pair, hand-stitched and with heels an inch and a half high, the thick soles studded with sharp iron spikes. They affected a colored sash and great, broad-brimmed hats. Dandies they were, half heroes and half devils when the excitement of the drink was in their veins.
> The duties of these men were often dangerous. To them belonged the breaking of the rollaways, riding on logs in the boiling river, shooting rapids, and sometimes in bravado making the log on which they stood spin in the water like a top. They camped at evening by a big fire on the river bank, with a rude shanty for their lodging, loved the

open air like gypsies, and led as free a life.

They were the terror of the small villages through which they passed. The marshal and his men were too weak to cope with them: but as they spent money freely, the saloon keeper was always on the watch to welcome them. And everywhere they went they found or made their share of boisterous fun.

William Chalmers Covert, a Presbyterian sky pilot, wrote *Glory of the Pines: A Tale of the Ontonagon* (Philadelphia, 1913), based on his experiences while serving a parish "hidden deep in the pine forests lying along the south shore of Lake Superior." The author much regretted that in his novel's plot "laid amidst the beauty and purity of the vast pine forest and under the clean skies of the North, sin - ugly sin - should have to make its mark." Despite his heavy-handed moralistic tone, Covert offers excellent word pictures of lumbering on the Ontonagon River. Consider his description of the start of a log run:

Above us we saw coming the on rush of water that had been set free at the dam. It was coming like a foam-topped tidal wave that had risen from somewhere out in the forest beauty and quiet and was sweeping everything before it, roaring through the echoing woods with the noise of a hurricane. The big logs from the dry sand bars, where they had hung for weeks, were picked up like matches and tossed into the current. When the water struck the gorge at the foot of which our camp was set, the fun began in earnest. The heavy cuts that had been picked from turns and shallows went booming and tumbling into the narrows, where, jammed together, they ground their rough sides as they fought in the fury of the stream. Long,

The Upper Tahquamenon Falls when pine was king.

stringy ribbons as well as huge sheets of brown bark ripped from the bruised logs went snapping through the air, and now and then a butt length, injured in the felling, split and went to pieces in the turmoil. When the end of a sixteen-foot log struck a pot hole in the floor of the gorge the huge "stick" flew clear of the water and went hurtling through the air. So often did we see this, that the cavorting timbers looked like huge water monsters at play in the frenzied flood, while the crunching and grinding on the rough sides of the dalles added to the suggestion of a battle of primeval brutes.

William D. Hulbert, the son of a lumberjack who in 1893 had moved his family to the western Chippewa County community named in his honor, was unable to follow his father's profession because he had been handicapped by polio as a child. However, he spent much of his childhood in the woods and at his father's saw mill and lumber camp. Based on those experiences he wrote a book of natural history essays *Forest Neighbors* (N.Y. 1902), and a series of articles that appeared in popular American magazines during the first decade of the 20th century. The Historical Society of Michigan republished nine of those articles as *White Pine Days on the Tahquamenon* in 1949. Hulbert's article, *With the Tahquamenon Drive*, which originally appeared in the *Outlook Magazine* in 1906, documents the thrilling breaking of a log jam on the very brink of the Upper Tahquamenon Falls:

A center jam formed just above the falls, only a few yards back from the verge, and to break it the men were obliged to get down into the water below it, stand there with the falls behind them and the current swirling about their knees, and pry the bottom logs out with their peavies. The water was not deep, and the jam itself sheltered them from the rush of the river, but if a man lost his footing he was gone. Carefully and cautiously they worked the first log loose, and as it started toward them they leaped upon it, and, before it could get away with them, jumped from it to the jam. But loosening one stick was not enough to start the rest, and they soon found that the whole pile would have to be torn apart little by little. More than that, other logs kept coming down the rapids and adding themselves to it, so that it grew at one end as rapidly as they could tear it away at the other; but they kept at it and in the course of time they worked back ten or twelve rods from the brink.

And then, of a sudden, one of them saw a long piece of pulpwood coming for him. There was no time for him to dodge, and it was too small to hold him if he mounted it, so, as the only chance he tried to jump over it. But it was too quick for him. It took him across the thighs, and the next instant he was down and the river was sweeping him towards the falls. On he went, faster and faster, nearer and nearer, till he was almost on the verge, and then, by some miracle of strength and agility, he got his spiked shoes against something solid, rose to his feet, and started to wade back against the current. Little by little he forged ahead till he met some logs large enough to carry his weight, and, mounting them, he jumped from one to another till he reached the jam. And then the foreman cursed him for having dropped his peavy, and he waded out again almost to the brink, found it where it had caught between some rocks, and brought it back.

The lumberjack novel that enjoyed the most

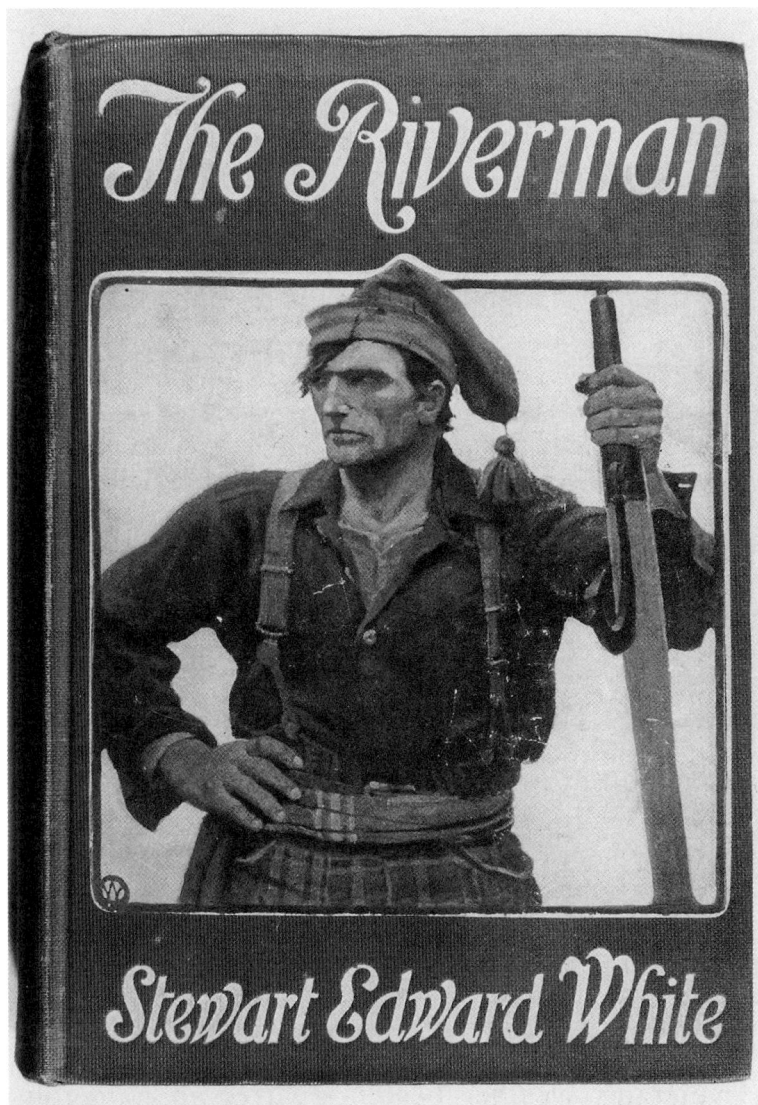

The Riverman published in 1908 featured artwork by N.C. Wyeth.

contemporary popularity and best glorified the drama of the river drive was Stewart Edward White's *The Riverman* (New York, 1908). Born in Grand Rapids in 1873, White lived during his childhood in a northern Michigan saw mill town, where he spent his days in the woods among the rivermen and in the lumber camps where his lumberjack father took him. His formal education began at Grand Rapids High School when he was 16. Two years later he graduated as class president and subsequently earned a BA and MA at the University of Michigan. He spent his summers adventuring on the Great Lakes and later prospected for gold in the Black Hills and worked in a Chicago slaughter house at $6 a week.

White wrote his first novel about Michigan lumbering, *The Blazed Trail*, (New York, 1902), set in the Saginaw River Valley and the Marquette vicinity, while working in a northern lumber camp. It established his literary career. His other books containing Michigan lumbering episodes include a collection of short stories originally appearing in magazines, *Blazed Trail Stories* (New York, 1904), a juvenile novel *The Adventures of Bobby Orde* (New York, 1908) and its sequel *The Rules of the Game* (New York, 1909). A prominent representative of the "red blood" school of fiction which glorified the manly qualities of laboring men, White produced nearly 50 volumes of fiction, travel, biography and spiritualism prior to his death in 1946. Set amid a western Michigan river drive during the 1870s, *The Riverman* offers a description of the activities of those folk heros:

This crew was forty in number, and had been picked from the best - a hard-bitten, tough band of veterans, weather beaten, scarred in numerous fights or by the backwoods scourge of small-pox, compact, muscular, fearless, loyal, cynically aloof

180

from those not of their cult, outspoken and free to criticize - in short, men to do great things under the strong leader, and to mutiny at the end of three days under the weak. They piled off the train at Sawyer's, stamped their feet on the board platform of the station, shouldered their "turkeys," and straggled off down the tote-road. It was an eighteen-mile walk in. The ground had loosened its frost. The footing was ankle-deep in mud and snow-water.

Next morning, bright and early, the breaking of the rollways began. During the winter the logs had been hauled down ice roads to the river, where they were "banked" in piles twenty, and even thirty, feet in height. The bed of the stream itself was filled with them for a mile, save in a narrow channel left down through the middle to allow for some flow of water; the banks were piled with them, side on, ready to roll down at the urging of the men.

First of all, the entire crew set itself, by means of its peavies, to rolling the lower logs into the current, where they were rapidly borne away. As the waters were now at flood, this was a quick and easy labor. Occasionally some tiers would be stuck together by ice, in which case considerable prying and heaving was necessary in order to crack them apart. But forty men, all busily at work, soon had the river full. Orde detailed some six or eight to drop below in order that the river might run clear to the next section, where the next crew would take up the task. These men, quite simply, walked to the edges of the rollway, rolled a log apiece into the water, stepped aboard, leaned against their peavies, and were swept away by the swift current. The logs on which they stood whirled in the eddies, caromed against other timbers, slackened speed, shot away; never did the riders

181

Lumberjack novelist George Wallace Skinner in the woods near Pellston in 1912.

alter their poses of easy equilibrium.

From time to time one propelled his craft ashore by hooking to and pushing against other logs. There he stood on some prominent point, leaning his chin contemplatively against the thick shaft of his peavy, watching the endless procession of the logs drifting by. Apparently he was idle, but in reality his eyes missed no shift of the ordered ranks. When a slight hitch or pause, a subtle change in the pattern of the brown carpet caught his attention, he sprang into life. Balancing his peavy across his body, he made his way by short dashes to the point of threatened congestion. There, working vigorously, swept down stream with the mass, he pulled, hauled and heaved, forcing the heavy, reluctant timbers from the cohesion that threatened trouble later. Oblivious to his surroundings, he wrenched and pried desperately. The banks of the river drifted by. Point succeeded point, as though withdrawn up stream by some invisible manipulator. The river appeared stationary, the banks in motion. Finally he heard at his elbow the voice of the man stationed below him, who had run out from his own point.

White's *The Blazed Trail* and *The Riverman* became best sellers, remaining in print for decades. But a number of other good novels about Michigan lumbering never enjoyed that success and as a result have become scarce, sought-after collector's items. Flint resident George Wallace Skinnner, who had worked as a youth in the lumber camps near Pellston in 1912, privately published *The Axe Thrower of the Tittabawassee* in 1935. The author actually printed and bound the small press run of his sole literary work. Though weak in plot and character development the volume provides rare and detailed descriptions of the technical aspects of lumbering. The hero of the story,

Dan Dell, a novice lumberjack who becomes an expert at the sport of ax throwing, participates in a variety of jobs in the woods. Assigned one day to the lowly but necessary task of "chickadee," Dan describes the process of making sleigh roads:

Dan had never seen such a road. He now saw how it was possible for teams to haul such great loads. The sleigh roads had first been opened and graded, even as a railroad grade, made as nearly level and straight as possible to build them, without too much cost. This grading had been done in the summer and fall, before the snow came, and now it was a picture, long stretches of beautiful roadways winding through the pines and cedars, cut and cleaned to a width of perhaps fifteen to eighteen feet. Then after the snow had fallen, which by now was something like twelve to eighteen inches upon the level, the teams had been sent through with the snow plows. These plows were heavy and had great spreading wings of oak plank. To the bottom edges of these wings were attached blades of steel which cut a sleek trough in the snow, throwing it up in great banks along either side, leaving two or three inches of snow lying in the trough's bottom, flat and smooth to a width of about seven feet.

After the roads had been thus plowed out, the sprinkler would go over it and thoroughly soak the bed with water. These sprinklers comprised a set of regular logging sleighs, being about six feet between the runners and very strong. A great box or tank was erected thereon, holding sixty to one hundred barrels of water. At the rear and directly above the track of each runner, and at the bottom of the tank, was bored a two inch hole. Into these holes were driven long plugs. When it was desired to release the water, the plugs were pulled out, allowing a great stream of water to flow out upon the road, which spread by the time it reached the snow sufficiently to cover the entire roadbed. Thus by driving repeatedly over the road for a few days during freezing weather, a thick layer of ice was formed.

Then another plow was put over the road, having short knives set at an angle to the bed so that a trench some fifteen or eighteen inches wide and two or three inches deep was formed for the sleigh runners to follow. Often these ice roads were yet in good condition for hauling late in the springtime, even after the snow was gone from the woods.

Among the scarcest of the lumberjack novels and a cut above most of the ilk in terms of colorful prose that captures the shanty boys' slang is *Nick of the Woods: A Tale of the Manistee* by Alaska Blacklock, a pseudonym of George Edward Lewis. A grandson of artist James Otto Lewis who painted portraits of Indian chiefs while a member of the 1826 Lewis Cass and Thomas McKenney expedition along the south shore of Lake Superior, Lewis was born in the Fife Lake vicinity in 1870. As a teenager he worked in northern Michigan Lumber camps prior to moving to Grand Rapids. During the early years of the 20th century he migrated to Alaska and ultimately Portland, Oregon, where his novel was published in a small edition in 1916. Set in lumber camps on the Manistee, Boardman, Au Sable and Muskegon rivers, the book offers choice descriptions of camp life, river runs and the felling of the pine:

The most interesting and entertaining part of the loggers' life was seen amid the tall and waving pine where they were the masters. Sawing, chopping, skidding, loading and swamping was their delight. Each was proud of his dexterity,

George Edward Lewis, alias Alaska Blacklock, wrote a novel and poetry about lumbering.

many a feat of skill and strength was exhibited. McQueen, with his timber cleaver weighing as it did two ounces over seven pounds, hung on a handle he had shaven from the trunk of a rock elm tree, would step up to a pine and darken the sun with chips, not an ax mark could be found on either stump or butt, so accomplished was he in his craft, the ply of that mighty ax, the magic of the deepening notch, made one feel that the tree was but wax and the ax-man a giant from some other world. The champion gang with the cross-cut were equipped with a seven foot Atkins saw, and on a wager for a new hat, pulled at the rapid rate of three strokes a second, and cut a thousand feet of logs in fifteen minutes. In this registered feat the Zip brothers have never been excelled.

Lewis also wrote verse, four volumes in all, including *Heart Echoes* and *The Poet's Idle Hour* published in Grand Rapids in the 1890s. An exceedingly rare pamphlet, *Jim*, published also in Grand Rapids in 1909, is his poetic tribute to a lumberjack who had saved his life 27 years before while the two were "cutting pine off Webb's hills, five miles east of Jam One, near where Canon Creek empties into the Manistee River:"

Bow-Legged Jim was a corker in camp.
He would drink like a fish and eat like a tramp.
He chewed tobacco, smoked Killikinick,
Played Seven-up and Sixty-six.
He could joke like Crockett, swear like Kidd.
But he never would do what the rules forbid.
When the fellows quarreled, Jim would joke,
The argument passed like a whiff of smoke.
When the boss was angry, Jim kept mum,
He was a favorite Lumber Jack chum.

Other lumberman chose the poetic genre to record their forest life. Perhaps the best known from Michigan was Douglas Malloch. Born in Muskegon in 1877, Malloch grew up in and graduated from high school in that rip-roaring lumber town. At the age of ten he published his first poem in the *Detroit News* and between 1906 and his death in 1938 he authored nine books of verse including *In Forest Land* (Chicago, 1906), *The Woods* (Chicago, 1913), and *Tote Road and Trail: Ballads of the Lumberjack* (Indianapolis, 1917). The latter volume contains "When the Drive Goes Down," typical of his rhythm and style:

> There's folks that like the good dry land,
> and folks that like the sea,
> But rock an' river, shoal an' sand,
> are good enough for me.
> There's folks that like the ocean crest,
> an' folks that like the town--
> But when I really feel the best
> is when the drive goes down.
> So pole away, you river rats,
> From landin' down to lake--
> There's miles of pine to keep in line,
> A hundred jams to break!

Judge George Angus Belding of Dearborn, spent his youth in a lumber camp near Onaway and worked as a lumberjack following service in World War I. In 1946 he published *Tales From the Presque Isle Woods*. It contains verse much superior to the usual "Vanity Press" publications. The poems were based on his childhood memories of "caulk-booted lumberjacks, vigorous, bearded fellows loping the limbs from the fallen trees, swamping, skidding, top loading, driving. Memories of old Onaway on a Saturday night, the streets swarming with rugged

188

Douglas Malloch's 1917 *Tote Road and Trail* contains this
illustration by Oliver Kemp.

fighting men swaggering and carousing." Belding's "Winter Day" captures the tumult of morning in the lumber camp:

I remember a morning in the days of long ago
Like a thousand others in a land of ice and snow;
I heard the woods' boss bellowing,
"Hit the deck! Daylight in the swamp!"
I saw sleepy men tumbling from straw-filled bunks;
Teamsters tramping in with lanterns lit; horses
Fed before the men; the big percherons;
Lumberjacks sullenly washing and cursing at the
Icy water barrel, cold to hard calloused hands.
Men pulling on "Soo" pants,
heavy woolen socks;
Finns, Frenchmen, Scotch,
steel-shod fighting cocks.
Clanging of iron on railroad iron-
"Come and get it!"

Several folklorists published volumes of lumberjack ballads collected in part from Michigan sources. Franz Rickaby spent seven years gathering material from "men who worked in the woods of Michigan, Wisconsin and Minnesota, mainly during the Golden Age of American Lumbering (1870-1900)" which he published as *Ballads and Songs of the Shanty-Boy* in 1926. Earl Clifton Beck, who managed lumber camps in the woods north of the Muskegon and Saginaw valleys for 20 years beginning in 1936, collected ballads and poems from the old timers published in 1941 as *Songs of the Michigan Lumberjacks* and in an enlarged version in 1948, *Lore of the Lumber Camps*. Michigan State University Professor Richard M. Dorson included a chapter on lumberjack folklore in his *Bloodstoppers and Bearwalkers* (Cambridge, 1952), based on stories he heard from authentic Upper Peninsula shanty boys.

Of the scores of Paul Bunyan books published since 1926 two in particular were based on Michigan sources. James Stevens wrote The *Saginaw Paul Bunyan* in 1932 and Sault Ste. Marie native Stan Newton produced *Paul Bunyan of the Great Lakes* in 1946.

And a few of the many histories of lumbering have been written by actual lumbermen. George W. Hotchkiss immigrated to Bay City in 1861 where he established a lucrative lumber barging enterprise. He also erected saw mills west of Bay City in 1864 and at Greenwood in Ogemaw County in 1871. He moved to Chicago in 1877 where he edited several lumber trade journals. In 1894 Hotchkiss produced a massive volume *Industrial Chicago: The Lumber Interests,* a biographical compendium of lumbermen of the Great Lakes region. Four years later he published his *History of the Lumber and Forest Industry of the Northwest,* which remains the most comprehensive volume on its subject.

Prior to his literary career Stewart H. Holbrook worked in lumber camps in New England and British Columbia before and after World War I. His first book, *Holy Old Mackinaw* (New York 1938), remains one of the most readable histories of the lumberjack and contains much of Michigan interest. Lewis C. Reimann published an account of his childhood days in Iron River, *Between the Iron and the Pine,* in 1951. He includes a chapter about his experiences working as a lumber camp cook's helper. He followed that volume with two others about Upper Peninsula lumbering *When Pine Was King* (1952) and *Incredible Seney* (1953).

And that brings us full circle back to the Seney Bar where the old lumberjack has recovered from his coughing spell, slugged down another shot and climbed back up on the table.

"Oh, those were glorious days when pine was

king - we thought they'd last forever - there was so much pine - we'd never cut it all - but we did! By the turn of century we were logging the last in the U.P. Where'd it all go? Well we built Chicago - twice! As well as many another town out on the treeless prairie."

"I sure do miss the sound of the wind sighing through those big trees - the smell of the pine pitch - the yell **timberrr!** What I wouldn't give to be able to sink this ax into a big old cork pine and send a chip flying the size of your head - but they're all gone now boys, they're all gone now."

Stove Maker to the Nation

Morning, noon and night millions of Victorian homemakers bent low, as if in supplication, before the huge, ornate wood-fired ranges that dominated their kitchens. On weekly baking days, their mutton-chop sleeved arms pulled plump loaves of golden bread from ovens. Early cold winter mornings generations of children donned their clothing while backed up to toasty wood burning stoves whose isinglass fronts cast a ruddy glow over the room.

Across America and elsewhere, more often than not, the ranges that baked the cake, fried the morning salt pork, bubbled the stew pot and heated Saturday night bath water and Monday's wash water originated in Michigan. In Detroit, Dowagiac, Kalamazoo, Battle Creek and other cities scattered across the peninsulas, thousands of skilled iron molders, sheet metal fitters, nickle platers and allied artisans fashioned the stoves that warmed the nation's behinds.

In 1905, Michigan Commissioner of Labor Malcolm J. McLeod boasted that: "Michigan is the greatest stove producing state in the world and her metropolis, Detroit, manufactures more stoves than any other city in the universe." Galactic hyperbole aside, Michigan was then indeed - stove maker to the nation!

The state's stove industry had originated in Detroit during the pioneer era of the 1830s. The center of the industry then lay in Albany and Troy, New York, and Michigan frontiersmen needing stove parts or repairs had to bear the expense, and months of wait, for delivery via the Erie Canal and Great Lakes ships. A pair of Detroit entrepreneurs named Kellogg and Van Schoick responded to that problem by founding the Hydraulic Iron Works that produced

Built in 1870, the Detroit Stove Company's factory sprawled along the river in Hamtramck.

replacement castings and repaired stoves.

Gradually the actual manufacture of stoves emerged as a sideline. By 1846, Harmon De Graff had also established a stove manufacturing facility in Detroit. His letterhead advertised he made "cooking, parlor, six plate, box and tight air stoves." The Rev. Albertus Van Raalte bought one of De Graff's stoves in December, 1846, and transported it to the incipient community of Holland, the Dutch colony he established the following month.

But it was the efforts of a young Hydraulics Iron Works apprentice named Jeremiah Dwyer that would lay the foundation for the preeminence of the Detroit stove industry. At the age of one, Dwyer had emigrated with his family from New York to Michigan in 1838. They pioneered a farm in Wayne County's Springwells Township. Ten years later Dwyer's father died when a passing locomotive spooked his team and he was thrown from the wagon. The family moved to Detroit and the teenaged Dwyer joined the work force to help support his siblings. Serving a four year apprenticeship with the Hydraulic Iron Works, he learned the skill of iron molding. Next he worked as a journeyman at several New York firms and then returned to Detroit to pursue his dream of manufacturing stoves on his own.

Finally in 1861, Dwyer, his brother James and Thomas W. Mizer succeeded in establishing the firm that ultimately became the Detroit Stove Works. The company's widely advertised "Jewel" brand stoves sold well. In 1870, Dwyer built a mammoth new factory in Hamtramck. By 1887, some 1,300 laborers converted 16,000 tons of iron annually into 60,000 stoves, available in an amazing 700 different models.

Dwyer had left the Detroit Stove Company in 1871 and in partnership with others started up the rival Michigan Stove Company. A work force numbering more than 1,000 by 1887 produced the

A turn-of-the-century Round Oak catalog featured gold miners warming themselves with the famous stove.

popular "Garland" line of stoves and ranges. At the factory on Jefferson Street a gigantic replica of a Garland range built for the Columbian Exposition stood as a familiar Detroit landmark for decades.

Brother James Dwyer was the spark plug behind the formation of the Peninsular Stove Company in 1881. During the 1880s the company manufactured some 270 different models of stoves at its "works" located at the corner of Fort and Eighth streets. Those big three Detroit stove makers were among the city's largest employers by the 1890s. In 1901 the Detroit factories employed over 3,500 workers who produced more than 300,000 stoves and ranges annually.

Factories situated away from Detroit's hubbub also added luster to Michigan's stove-making reputation. In 1847 Ezra Wilder, an entrepreneur from New York state, built a blast furnace in Kalamazoo to process the nearby large deposits of bog iron, a sedimentary deposit resulting from iron rich water percolating through the soil. He went broke in the attempt but two local men, Allen Potter and Jeremiah Woodbury, bought the furnace, and established a stove factory to utilize the pig iron produced. By 1853 the Potter and Woodbury blast furnace was the largest in the state. They sold out the following year to William Burtt who continued to expand the operation. In 1855, Burtt's work force of 25 stove makers converted 500 tons of iron into 4,500 parlor, box and cooking stoves. Kalamazoo's bog iron industries flourished throughout the 1850s but ultimately lost out to competion elsewhere in the state.

In 1854, Philo D. Beckwith, set up a blacksmith shop in the little Cass County community of Dowagiac that grew up along the recently completed Michigan Central Railroad tracks. A few years later he invented an improved "under-draft" wood burning stove to heat his shop. Michigan Central Railroad

The mythical Chief Doe-Wah-Jack promoted Round Oak
stoves.

officials admired the superior heating qualities of the similar stove Beckwith had installed in the local depot and ordered more.

Thus began the company that would become Dowagiac's major employer for decades. By 1868, Beckwith had constructed a factory adjacent the railroad tracks. Production of his "Round Oak" stoves boomed and Dowagiac soon billed itself as "the Furnace City of America." In 1899 an army of laborers 1,500 strong timed their days to the deep bass voice of the Round Oak Stove Company whistle heard in four adjacent counties. At the massive stove works sparwled over 15 acres in the heart of the city, workers cast 40 tons of pig iron a day into fire pots, shaped boiler plate into stove bodies and added as a finishing touch finely worked, nickle-platted fittings. In 1925 the company boasted that over two million of its Round Oak stoves and kitchen ranges were in use across the land. Ultimately over 400 other manufacturers would emulate the Round Oak line.

Advertising proved an important aspect of the Round Oak Company's success. Beginning in 1905 the company adopted as its trademark a mythical Indian chief it named "Doe-Wah-Jack." Colorful calendars and catalogs depicting the chief single-handedly fighting bears and in other ticklish situations, souvenir spoons, plates, steins and his nickle-plated visage mounted on stove parts made Doe-Wah-Jack nearly as familiar to Americans as the Indian on the buffalo nickel.

A Kalamazoo manufacturer parlayed its own unique advertising campaigns into an equally successful operation. Founded in 1901 by a coterie of businessmen previously involved in the industry in Detroit, the Kalamazoo Stove Company sought to eliminate the middleman and market its products directly to consumers,. The company unveiled its line of steel ranges, steel cookstoves and "an oak heater,"

The Depression era Kalamazoo Stove Co. catalog promoted its huge work force.

under the initial slogan "seeing is believing; trying makes believing doubly sure." The Kalamazoo Stove Company sold $200,000 worth of stoves by the close of 1903. Then their advertising genius, Marco Morrow, came up with "From Kalamazoo Direct to You!"

Next to celery, the crunchy vegetable which first made Kalamazoo a household word, that phrase probably did more than anything else to popularize the city's name. Soon thousands of people across the nation were chanting the catchy phrase and filling out order blanks for the stoves. Kalamazoo stoves proved superior products and they included innovations such as thermometers mounted on the oven door and glass windows which first allowed cooks to view the interior of the oven without opening it.

Hard pressed to keep up with production orders, the company grew lustily even throughout the Depression. During the 1930s the Kalamazoo Stove Company's foundries, tinshops, enamel plant and other operations covered a 20 acre tract where 2,000 employees crafted more than 200 styles of stoves, ranges and furances. More than 300 factory branches across the nation served as showrooms and retail outlets. By the decade's end families encompassing a total of more than 12,000 people depended on the Kalamazoo Stove Company for their livelihood. By that time, however, the name of a new model of furnace unveiled in 1934, the "Dictator," would not seem so appealing.

Stove companies also formed an important element of the economy of other southwestern Michigan communities. Nearby Battle Creek, "the Cereal City to the Nation," entered the stove making sweepstakes in 1909 when the Grand Rapids Stove Company moved there and reorganized as the A-B Stove Company. Using the slogans "Not How Cheap - But How Good" and "As Easy to Clean as a China

NOT HOW CHEAP—BUT HOW GOOD

A-B Gas Ranges
The Finest Gas Range in the World

No. 44.   A-B Full Tile Range
A Model of Compactness and Efficient Cooking
Equipment
Sanitary—Economical—Convenient—Beautiful
A-B STOVE COMPANY, BATTLE CREEK, MICH.

AS EASY TO CLEAN AS A CHINA PLATE

Cook books distributed by Battle Creek's A-B Stove Co. in 1911 included plenty of advertisements.

Plate," the A-B Company specialized in gas ranges and gas hot water heaters and later expanded into production of electric ranges. In 1911 the company began issuing popular recipe books that promoted the use of "scientific cooking" via its more hygenic products.

The Ottawa County community of Holland received a major economic boost in 1906 when John P. Kolla and A.H. Landwehr launched the Holland Furnace Company. Production of its massive central heating units expanded rapidly. Emulating the Kalamazoo Stove Company's marketing concepts, the Holland Furnace Company established a system of 500 factory branches located in 44 states. Its popular slogan "Holland furnaces make warm friends," a promotional team of miniature draught ponies and other advertising gimmicks helped build a national reputation. By the 1920s the company had become "the world's largest installers of home heating and air conditioning systems," and Holland's major employer.

The gradual obsolence of wood burning stoves posed problems for Michigan manufacturers but most of the companies continued remarkably strong through the Depression years by adding gas and electric models to their lines. But World War II brought a bigger threat to the industry. Shortly after mobilization the government ordered production halted in all stove companies with an annual volume in excess of $2 million. Many of the plants converted to manufacturing military needs. The Kalamazoo Stove Company, for example, turned to making it hot for the enemy as expert stove makers fashioned parachute flares, armor plate for tanks, and landing gear for warplanes.

Reconversion after the war, however, proved a particularly tough problem because production facilities had been so drastically altered. Retooling appeared to be too expensive a proposition. The

Kalamazoo Stove Company would not survive the 1950s.

The Michigan Stove Company and the Detroit Stove Company had merged by the late 1930s. In 1945, Battle Creek's A-B Stove Company also joined the corporation and in 1953 the entire operation moved to Detroit. But four years later all three closed their doors forever. The Round Oak Stove Company also went out of business about that time. The Holland Furnace Company limped along under financial contraints into the 1960s when it was purchased by a New Jersey company and the Holland plant closed.

The demise of the Michigan stove and furnace dynasties brought hardship to the various cities where their massive factories sprawled. But those communities survived and eventually something else emerged to take up the economic slack. Industrial evolution has been part and parcel of Michigan's diverse economy since territorial days. Perhaps the story of the rise and fall of the stove industry holds lessons for Michigan's future during the continuing cycle of factory closings and industrial relocation.

Gen. Custer, Capt. Glazier
& Paul Revere

Astride his spirited Kentucky thoroughbred, Paul Revere, Civil War cavalry veteran and popular author Willard Glazier clomped along the dusty main street of Euclid, Ohio. He found the usually quiet community abuzz with excitement, but not over his arrival nor through residual jollity about the gala 1876 Centennial Fourth of July celebration of two days before. It was news from Montana that had the Euclidians so stirred up - the first startling rumors that the Sioux had massacred Gen. George Armstrong Custer and his entire command.

Because of his "long association with the general during the Civil War," Glazier took the thought of Custer's death "very much to heart." Custer, a dashing and flamboyant cavalryman, had distinguished himself through his bravery during the war, winning promotion to general at the age of 23. Despite his many fierce cavalry charges against sometimes overwhelming Confederate forces and subsequent warfare with hostile Indians out west, his life had seemed charmed. Eleven times horses had been shot out from under him and he had been wounded only once. Could it be that Custer's luck had finally run out?

During the following two weeks as Glazier tarried in Cleveland and Toledo, the shocking rumors were confirmed. The Battle of the Little Big Horn and Custer's Last Stand became permanently enshrined in American popular culture.

Glazier, had cantered out of Boston on May 9, 1876, intent on making an equestrian tour from ocean to ocean, visiting army buddies en route and lecturing on "The Heroes of the Revolution" to raise money for the Grand Army of the Republic (G.A.R.) relief

Gen. George Armstong Custer grew up in Monroe.

fund for widows and orphans. The old cavalryman decided to deviate from his planned itinerary and swing north through Michigan so that he could visit Custer's hometown, Monroe, and learn more about his departed hero.

Glazier had launched his literary career in 1865 with *The Capture The Prison Pen and The Escape,* which, he claimed, sold 400,000 copies and made him a small fortune. He followed that best seller with other books based on his Civil War experiences including, *Three Years in the Federal Cavalry* (1870) and *Battles for the Union* (1874). As his books testified, Glazier experienced numerous thrilling adventures but he clearly lacked Custer's luck. His fate was to be repeatedly captured and incarcerated.

Born in Fowler, New York, in 1841, Glazier grew up on a nearby farm. Following graduation from the state normal school in Albany he taught for two years. When the war broke out in 1861, Glazier enlisted as a private in the 2nd New York Cavalry. By September, 1863, he had earned promotion to first lieutenant. He first met Custer on September 12, 1863, at the third Battle of Brandy Station, Virginia, the largest cavalry engagement of the war. Glazier wrote:

Custer had but recently been commissioned brigader-general and this was the first time he went into action at the head of his brigade. His appearance was very conspicuous. A mere boy in years, gorgeously equipped, in short, bearing upon his person all the gold lace and other paraphernalia allowed his rank, he formed a striking figure - such a one as is seldom seen on the battlefield. His arrival at Brandy Station was at a critical juncture, and while we were momentarily expecting a conflict with (Gen. J.E.B.) Stuart's cavalry, then directly in our front, all had a curiosity to see how the gaily dressed brigadier would acquit himself. It seemed to be the general impression that he would not have the nerve to "face the music" with his band box equipment, but he soon proved himself equal to the occasion. Being ordered to charge the enemy, he snatched his cap from his head, handed it to his orderly, drew his sword and dashed to the front of his brigade, then formed in column of squadrons. The command "Forward!" was instantly given. A moment later "Trot!" was sounded; then "Gallop!" and "Charge!" and before the Confederates had time to realize that we really intended an attack, they were swept from the field, and a section of a battery with which they had been opposing our advance was in the possession of the young general and his gallant cavalrymen. No soldier who saw him on that day at Brandy Station ever questioned his right to a star, or all the gold lace he felt inclined to wear.

Glazier saw Custer numerous times during the succeeding month. But on October 19th near Buckland Mills, Virginia, Glazier's horse was shot out from under him. Injured by the fall, Glazier lay on the battlefield while the hooves of the charging Confederate cavalry trammeled his body into the mud. He regained consciousness while being carried from the field as a Confederate prisoner. He spent the next 14 months suffering brutal treatment as a prisioner of war, stationed first at the infamous Libby Prison at Richmond, Virginia, then at stockades in Danville, Georgia; and Charleston and Columbia, South Carolina. Glazier and a companion escaped from the stockade at Columbia, but after eluding hounds, alligators and Confederate soldiers for three weeks the cavalrymen were recaptured by a Rebel picket. A few days later Glazier got away again briefly before being caught by a troop of Texas Rangers. At Sylvania, Georgia, he succeeded in breaking free again and this

Capt. Glazier was taken prisoner in 1863 when his horse was shot from under him.

time found his way to the Union lines. His term of enlistment had expired by then, and Glazier returned home for two months of recuperation. He then reenlisted in the 26th New York Cavalry with whom he served the remainder of the war, reaching the rank of captain.

Following his discharge Glazier began carving out his career as "soldier author." He also joined the G.A.R., membership in which was *sine qua non* for any writer intent on selling his books to Union veterans. Glazier's 1876 equestrian tour across the continent came under the auspices of the G.A.R., credentials which secured him a hearty reception in the communities he visited.

Despite the "advance man" hired to drum up enthusiasm for Glazier's lectures, he was surprised to find a larger than usual crowd assembled at the outskirts of Custer's hometown as he rode into Monroe on July 24, 1876. Accompanied by a brass band, the citizens escorted the cavalryman to the city hall where the hastily formed Custer Monument Association received him.

Glazier agreed to postpone his lecture for three days to give the association an opportunity to better advertise it. And he announced his decision to donate the proceeds from that and all his Michigan appearances toward their goal of erecting an equestrian statue of Custer.

Glazier devoted his three days in Monroe to learning more about the fallen general. He visited with Custer's father who gave him a tour of the family home, ironically filled with Indian souvenirs, and he met some of the general's boyhood friends. He learned that Custer had moved to Monroe at the age of ten to live with his married half sister. Shortly thereafter he met a pretty little brown-eyed girl, Elizabeth Bacon, the daughter of a local judge. It was love at first sight and in 1864 they married. Libbie

Custer would devote the remainder of her life defending her husband's memory following his death at the controversial Battle of the Little Big Horn.

From Monroe, Glazier rode to Detroit, spending a night en route at Ecorse. He found the scenery at the "City of the Strait" a far cry from that of today. Glazier observed "in every direction it is brightened by parks and adorned by fountains; and the broad avenues lined by generous borders of grass and shaded by cool lines of trees, are something for Americans to be proud of..." Following a successful lecture at Detroit, Glazier headed for his next scheduled appearance at Ypsilanti, then made brief stops at Ann Arbor, Dexter, Chelsea, and Grass Lake before pushing on to Jackson.

After enjoying another well attended lecture in Jackson, Glazier rode to Battle Creek, stopping for meals at Parma, Albion and Marshall. Eugene T. Freeman, a fellow G.A.R. member, introduced Glazier to his Battle Creek audience. Freeman, who had enlisted as a corporal in the 20th Michigan Infantry at Battle Creek in 1862 and ultimately transferred to a New York artillery battery to accept promotion to second lieutenant, struck up a friendship with Glazier. He took him to his church the next morning and in the afternoon they enjoyed a buggy ride to Goguac Lake.

The following day found Glazier in Kalamazoo, then popularly known as "The Big Village." Not until 1884 would that community, whose 18,000 residents Glazier thought "perfectly alive," change from its village status to that of a city. Following his lecture to a full house in Kalamazoo, Glazier met two residents of particular interest. Maj. R.F. Judson, an attorney who resided on Asylum Avenue, as Oakland Avenue was known until a local real estate promoter sought a better image for his holdings, had served as an aide to Custer when he commanded the famous Michigan Cavalry Brigade. From Judson Glazier

Capt. Willard Glazier, the "soldier writer."

learned additional details about the general's courage and skill during the war.

While in Kalamazoo Glazier also paid a visit to Col. Frederick W. Curtenius. A banker and official of the State Hospital at that time, Curtenius had led a colorful life. Born in New York in 1806, the son of a general in the War of 1812, Curtenius had graduated from Hamilton College in 1823. He studied law for a while, but finding the military profession more appealing he sailed to South America and fought in Columbia under Simon Bolivar "to help free them from the yoke of Spain." In 1835 Curtenius immigrated to Kalamazoo County where he became a pioneer farmer. Twelve years later he raised a company of the 1st Michigan Infantry and as captain he fought in the Mexican War.

When the Civil War broke out in 1861, Curtenius became colonel of the Sixth Michigan Infantry, serving in Louisiana. But an incident in June, 1862, would end his distinguished military career. Some runaway slaves had taken refuge behind the Union lines in Baton Rouge. Curtenius' commander, Gen. Thomas Williams, ordered him to return the "contraband" to their owners. The colonel refused, replying that he had not been commissioned by the state of Michigan to return slaves to their masters. Williams had him arrested for disobeying an order. Curtenius resigned his commission in disgust, was honorably discharged and returned to Kalamazoo. The state of Michigan upheld Curtenius' action and officially rebuked Williams, who unfortunately was killed in battle the following August. Curtenius continued his public service after the war, serving as a state senator in 1867-68 and for several terms as president of Kalamazoo.

En route to Kalamazoo Glazier's horse, Paul Revere, had developed a nasty saddle sore, So he shipped him to an old comrade in Michigan City for treatment and while awaiting the outcome took the train to Albion and Marshall where he delivered lectures. Next he made a return engagement to Battle Creek. Paul was shipped back to him there and Glazier continued his ride to the west.

At Comstock the old cavalryman experienced a close brush with disaster. His spirited horse became frightened by a passing Michigan Central train and leaped 40 feet down the river embankment, leaving Glazier and the saddle in the road. Stunned, though not seriously injured, Glazier recovered Paul who was quietly standing in the middle of the stream.

That incident and a hot 14 mile ride from Kalamazoo to Paw Paw aggravated Paul's condition. Glazier put his steed under the care of a Van Buren County farrier and registered at Paw Paw's Dyckman House. During the succeeding two weeks Glazier made that hotel and the Duncombe House in Decatur his headquarters while he made railroad forays to deliver lectures in Grand Rapids, Niles, South Bend, Michigan City and La Porte.

Glazier enjoyed his forced stay in Van Buren County. He wrote that "the people of Paw Paw were very kind, making the time pass agreeably and giving me a pleasant recollection to take away." At Decatur's sole hotel Glazier found comfortable lodging and he "thanked my stars that I was not stranded in some little backwoods place." The hospitality of Decatur residents also impressed him. He commented "No sooner had I reached Decatur than I lost the consciousness of being 'a stranger within the gates,' having been so cordially made to feel that I was among friends."

While at the Duncombe House, George L. Darby, a fellow member of the 2nd New York Cavalry and POW, noticed Glazier's name on the hotel register. The two enjoyed many hours of reminiscing when Darby took him on a fishing trip to nearby Lake

Glazier gives Paul Revere a rest while he records his day's activities.

of the Woods.

In addition to the Centennial celebration and Custer's last stand, 1876 witnessed the presidential campaign that pitted Ohio Republican Rutherford B. Hayes against Samuel J. Tilden of New York. This would become the notorious "disputed election," in which Tilden was denied his popular and electoral majority when Republican controlled election boards disallowed votes from key southern states. While lodged at the Duncombe House Glazier had an opportunity to witness the campaign heating up in Michigan. He wrote:

This was a great day for Decatur. With the morning came the completion of arrangements for a Republican mass meeting, and a rustic band from an adjacent village arrived at nine o'clock in a farm wagon. The "Stars and Stripes" floated majestically over the heads of the patriotic musicians, and the people were drawn from every quarter to the stirring call of fife and drum, eager to see their leaders and to listen to their views upon the vital questions of the day. The 'Silver Cornet Band' of Dowagiac cooperated with the Decatur Fife and Drum Corps,' in rousing the dormant element of the place, and, as its imposing appellation would imply, did so with dignified and classical selections. By nightfall the place was the scene of great activity, and to an onlooker produced a singular effect. Men were collected in groups engaged in excited conversation, torches flared in every direction, while at brief intervals voices were drowned in some lively tune from the silver cornets or the fife and drum.

Glazier lectured to a packed house in Decatur's Union Hall on the evening of September 4th and early the next morning he mounted his now healed horse.

216

Turning his "back upon the hospitable little village in which I spent so many pleasant days, and where I felt that I had indeed made many friends," he headed southwest, spending nights in Dowagiac, Niles and Buchanan. As Glazier left Buchanan he "could not avoid a certain feeling of regret that this was to be my last halt in the great state through which I had made such a pleasant and profitable journey."

After he crossed the state line Glazier found life among the Hoosiers considerably less to his liking. While en route to Michgan City he complained: "I am sorry to say that during this day's ride I encountered the worst roads and the dullest people of my journey." His inability to get proper directions from various Indiana citizens led Glazier to add: "Many who have resided in this part of Indiana for thirty and even forty years are not only exceedingly illiterate, but know much less of the topography of the country than the average Indian - and absolutely nothing of the adjacent towns."

Glazier experienced numerous adventures as he continued his ride across the continent, highlighted by his capture by a band of Arapaho Indian raiders near Cheyenne, Wyoming. The cavalryman with a penchant for getting captured managed to escape but not before he witnessed the torture and murder of a cowboy traveling with him. Glazier reached San Francisco without getting captured again and he terminated his 200 day ride by walking his faithful mount into the Pacific Ocean surf.

Glazier had planned to put together a book about his transcontinental exploit, but as frequently happens with authors, other projects intervened. In 1881, he made a 3,000 mile canoe voyage down the course of the Mississippi. During that adventure he discovered a small body of water in Minnesota he named Lake Glazier. He would write two books about his Mississippi trip in which he sought to prove

The Custer Memorial Statue erected in Monroe in 1910.

Lake Glazier was the true source of the Mississippi River, a claim that was ultimately disproved. He also found time to write *Heroes of Three Wars* (1878) and *Peculiarities of American Cities* (1883). Although John Owens included information about portions of the equestrian trek in his biography of Glazier, *Sword and Pen* (1880), not until 1896 would Glazier get around to publishing *Ocean to Ocean on Horseback*. It would be the last of his nine books. He died in 1905.

Despite the boost Glazier had given the Custer Memorial Association through his Michigan lecture proceeds, not until June 4, 1910, would Libbie Custer be able to unveil the huge equestrian statue of her lamented husband that had been funded by a $25,000 state appropriation. There at a conspicuous location on the bank of the River Raisin the bronze Custer continues to greet visitors to Monroe, his childhood home.

When Michigan
Girdled the Globe

Thronging city streets, park paths and bathing beaches, Gibson girls were all the rage. Whether sedately strolling, driving spirited teams or seated on "wheels,"as bicycles were then called, the voluptuous femme fatales sported luxuriant locks and perfect hourglass figures. It was the golden era of feminine pulchritude and the 18-inch-waist was the epitome of fashion.

The only problem in achieving the form so praised by poets, painters and playwrights lay in the fact that few women were actually shaped like an hourglass. No matter - what nature had not endowed could be achieved through artifice. And in that late Victorian era no woman, whether she be a humble chamber maid or Queen Victoria herself, dared venture forth into polite society unless securely bolstered in a corset.

But, like a tube of toothpaste squeezed hard in the middle, something had to give. Medical authorities had been warning women for generations that tight-laced corsets mortified their internal organs. The human body was not made to be thusly constructed, to be entombed! To demonstrate, one physician laced up a monkey in a corset - and it died in a manner of minutes.

Colorful Dr. James M. Peebles, a rascally "psychic healer" from Battle Creek wrote:

Corsets are curses. They produce the wasp-like waist, and the wasp is both the meanest and most ill-shaped insect that lives. Had I the power, I would seize with a pair of tongs every corset on earth and make one great pyramid pile, and applying the torch, I would burn them to ashes and

The famed hourglass figure was achieved through artifice.

dance the highland-fling over their ashes. There young lady! Now go and pout - and later repent, and reform, or die prematurely. If dying, let this be carved on your tombstone.

"Suicided With The Corset"

Few women, if any, responded to the likes of Peebles' picturesque rhetoric or to simian examples. They continued to heed fashion's dictates. Besides, scores of patent medicine makers proudly bottled preparations guaranteed to cure diverse female ailments, including conditions aggravated by tight lacing. From Kalamazoo, for example, distinguished Dr. Richard Pengelly and his matronly wife Mary proffered *Zoa Phora,* "Women's Friend." That Mary had founded the local Women's Christian Temperance Union did not prevent the couple from incorporating a generous dollop of alcohol into their panacea. Such nostrums often contained as much as 40% alcohol, narcotics or both. Needless to say, a slug of *Zoa Phora* made corset wearing considerably less painful - some women felt no pain at all!

Long before automobiles dominated Michigan's economy, factories in Detroit, Ann Arbor, Jackson, Kalamazoo and Saginaw annually produced millions of corsets. In 1910 the federal census taker found Michigan businesses the nation's second leading employer of corset workers. Women comprised nearly 90% of the corset labor force then - not only because they were more skilled in the sewing required in the trade but also because manufacturers could get away with paying them an average of $1.10 per ten-hour workday - less than half what their male counterparts earned. And women worked hard for their pittance.

Corset making involved as many as 40 specialized operations requiring varying degrees of skill and endurance. Women cut material, ran industrial

These turn of the century Kalamazoo Corset Company employees worked long hours for little pay.

sewing machines and stitched by hand. They joined seams, attached front clasps and back stitching, inserted steel wires and boning, sewed eyelets and added draw strings, lace embroidery, or flossing. Others ironed corsets, tied little bows and sewed them on, placed hooks, eyes and lacing, joined the two corset halves and packed the finished product for shipment across the nation.

Why Michigan attained such prominence in the corset industry is a matter of conjecture. Geography undoubtedly played an important role - all corset manufacturing sites, with the exception of a small operation in Saginaw, lay on the Michigan Central Railroad, a vital link to eastern and western markets. Perhaps also, the establishment of Jackson's Bortree Corset Company in 1871, the first such factory west of Boston, seeded interest in the industry. The Bortree Company specialized in its famous adjustable "Duplex Corset," "a time tried and unfailing favorite of millions." The success of Bortree's product, which the company boasted in 1889, "is worn wherever civilized woman is found," ultimately inspired 16 rival firms to establish factories in Jackson. Factories producing corset components also sprang up there. The Jackson Corset Steel Works, for example, in 1888 manufactured 33,750 gross pairs of its product, used to fasten together corset halves. If lined end to end, that output, a writer for the *Jackson Daily Citizen* computed, would stretch from Jackson to Chicago. During the 1880s alone, the Coronet Corset Co, the Jackson Corset Co. and the smaller Reliance Corset Company began shipping their torso-taming wares from Jackson.

Reliance was a good name for a corset - because countless millions of Victorian ladies relied on their corsets to preserve their figures, often under trying circumstances. Corsets sometimes failed because of the nature of the material used in the

AMERICAN BEAUTY CORSETS

are charmingly attractive garments that produce that prepossessing characteristic known as—STYLE.

These corsets at $1.00 and upwards are within reach of everyone.

Exclusively made by

Kalamazoo Corset Company

Sold by

All First Class Dealers

The Kalamazoo Corset Company targeted Western Normal Co-eds in this 1911 advertisement.

"stays" that strengthened the garment - whalebone. Pliable and strong when fresh, whalebone grew brittle with age. A sickening sound like small bones being broken startled more than one matron displaying a perfect hourglass figure when during the excitement of the dance she swooped to low. Her dance partner could not help but notice that upon straightening up - the sand in her hourglass had all but run out.

Beyond breaking at inopportune times, whalebone posed other problems. As whalers harpooned their quarry to near extinction whalebone, correctly termed baleen, grew more and more expensive. Then too, as Victorians crammed themselves into crowded church pews during the summer months, in the days before air conditioning, the substance had a tendency to give off somewhat of a fishy odor - a trait which did little to enhance the long-winded sermons then in vogue.

Edward K. Warren, a store keeper with an inventive knack from the Berrien County community of Three Oaks, sought to address the whalebone problem. Following a visit to a Chicago feather duster factory where he saw great piles of turkey feathers being discarded he got a brainstorm. In 1883, he patented a substitute produced from splintered turkey feathers which he dubbed "featherbone." He make a fortune via the large factories he built to manufacture his innovation, put the tiny town of Three Oaks on the map and ultimately got his own name on the Michigan map in the form of the Warren Dunes State Park on southern Lake Michigan.

One of Warren's employees, James H. Hatfield, launched a related venture, the Featherbone Corset Company, in 1891. A few years later Hatfield moved his operation to Kalamazoo where it evolved into the Kalamazoo Corset Company By the first decade of the 20th century the factory at the northeast corner of Eleanor and Church streets had emerged as the

Kalamazoo's Grace Corset Co. promoted its Madame Grace
line in 1915.

nation's largest corset producer - where more than 800 local ladies labored their ten-hour days, amid the machine gun chatter of hundreds of sewing machines, to produce the instruments of torture so desired by their countrywomen.

The Kalamazoo Corset Company experienced a bitter labor strike over more pay and better working conditions in 1912. Feminine picketers with the effrontery to also "throw men out of work" divided the Kalamazoo community for three and a half months before the strike ended with negligible gains by the International Ladies Garment Workers Union. Two years later Hatfield reorganized his giant company to unveil new lines of "Madame Grace" "American Beauty" and "La Mode" corsets. He later formed another firm, the National Corset Company. In 1915 Kalamazoo Corset Company advertising promised customers that whatever their varying figure requirements they could "select a Madam Grace corset that is to your intimate liking and which will give your figure the style lines required by the vogues of Spring and Summer."

Other Michigan corset manufacturers included Kalamazoo's Puritan Corset Company and Ann Arbor's The Crescent Works, both smaller concerns. Vying with the Kalamazoo Corset Company in size was Detroit's American Lady Corset Company established in 1895. In 1907, 814 women and 116 men found employment at its huge West Fort Street factory. The first decade of the 20th century also saw additional firms formed in Jackson including S.H. Camp and Company and the M & K Corset Company which ultimately became the Kellogg Corset Company under the management of Douglas C. Kellogg.

An unrelated namesake, Dr. John Harvey Kellogg, the flamboyant proprietor of the Battle Creek Sanitarium had long railed against the evils of tight-

A demure miss models her indispensable corset in 1915.

lacing. Nevertheless, he jumped on the fashion band wagon in 1902 and he promoted in the pages of his *Good Health* magazine the "Good Health adjustable waist," which laced up very much like a corset to produce the desired hourglass figure. Needless to say Kellogg is best remembered for his health food inventions -granola, peanut butter and corn flakes.

In 1907 alone, seven of the state's manufacturers, produced more than 4,250,000 corsets - enough to literally girdle the globe! Michigan's mighty corset makers remained strong through World War I. Then came a devastating development that brought the industry to its knees almost overnight - a revolution in fashion. Out went the hourglass figure, long dresses and long tresses - in came the boyish look of the "roaring 20s," flappers, bobbed hair and waist-less dresses. Most corset makers soon went "belly up" but some managed to survive the fashion blow under straitened circumstances by catering to those whose need for girdling outstripped sartorial demands.

But corsets went the way of the hoop skirt and bustle, mutton chop sleeves, high button shoes and other once popular relics.

And while thousands of Michigan women no longer hold jobs in corset factories, at least their descendants can breath easier.

The Acropolis of Kalamazoo:
The Birth of a Campus

"Kalamazoo is more tickled than the boy with his first pair of red top boots," wrote the editor of the Niles *Daily Star* on August 31, 1903. His comment concerned the State Board of Education's final decision to locate the new normal school in Kalamazoo. More than a hint of sour grapes tinted his analogy. Niles and some thirty other western Michigan cities and town had vied for the potentially lucrative prize. Kalamazoo's other chief rivals had been Allegan, Muskegon, Grand Rapids, Decatur, Three Oaks and Hastings. The story of how the Celery City won out and of how the institution that would become Western Michigan University survived its formative years is worth the telling.

Michigan, a pioneer in many aspects of American education, had taken a lead in the creation of teacher's training schools, or "normals" as they were called. Michigan State Normal School at Ypsilanti, now Eastern Michigan University, became the first such institution west of the Alleghany Mountains in 1853. Curiously enough, during the competition for this first normal one of the most elaborate papers delivered to the State Board of Education came from a committee of citizens in Kalamazoo County's Gull Prairie, now Richland.

Despite that early boost, Ypsilanti remained the only teacher training school in Michigan for over four decades. Finally, the growing need for similar institutions in other sections of the state resulted in the creation of Central State Normal School at Mount Pleasant in 1895 and Northern State Normal School at Marquette in 1899.

Western Michigan, comprising 17 counties with 25 percent of the state's population, urgently wanted its own normal. But the establishment of any type of state institution in those days was a plum to be picked only through adroit political maneuvering.

In 1901 Representative Luke Luggers of Holland introduced a bill calling for the establishment of a new normal school. The bill passed the Michigan House and Senate but Governor Aaron T. Bliss vetoed it. During the 1903 lawmaking session Representative Henry B. Vandercook of Grand Rapids assisted by Senator William D. Kelly of Muskegon renewed the fight for a Western State Normal School. Vandercook, who had grown up in Allegan and later became a successful Grand Rapids attorney, marshalled all his forces to subdue bitter opposition in the committees on education and ways and means. On May 27, 1903, Bliss signed Public Act No. 196, creating the "Western State Normal School."

The act included a less than modest appropriation of $37,001. The State Legislature allocated $25,000 for construction of a suitable building, $5,000 for equipment, $7,000 for the first year's salaries, and $1 for acquisition of a tract of land of at least 20 acres. Obviously the legislature intended the financing of the new normal school to be substantially augmented by the fortunate community chosen as the site.

Kalamazoo acted quickly. Not since the 1850s, when the community, than a village, had pulled off the coup of landing the new Asylum for the Insane had such an alluring prize seemed within reach. Civic and business leaders formed an organization called the Press Club, the original nucleus of what later became the Kalamazoo Chamber of Commerce, to organize the campaign. On June 3, 1903, one week after passage of the bill, the Press Club held a meeting to begin the drive. The City Council and local Board of Education attended. Following the meeting Mayor Sam Folz and President of the School Board Nathaniel H. Stewart spearheaded the local excitement as the group hurriedly secured options on 24 tracts of land in and near the city.

Kalamazoo stood ready when members of the State Board of Education made their first inspection visit. Civic leaders outlined Kalamazoo's long established cultural and educational traditions, its ample transportation facilities and central location in the region. But more tangible financial allurements caught the board's fancy. Not only would Kalamazoo be willing to donate any of the 24 available tracts of land but it would also hand the state $40,000 for building and developing the campus. In addition, the city would grade the streets and lay cement sidewalks adjacent to the sites, install gas, electricity, sewer and water hookups free, allow use of the public school buildings until the state could construct a training school and even pay half the salaries of the teachers at the new normal.

Other cities in western Michigan offered varying inducements but none so comprehensive as Kalamazoo's. On August 28, the board met to vote on a site. After 14 ballots and no result, the next tally proved decisive - Kalamazoo had won. "It is money that gets the school," grumbled the editor of the Niles *Daily Star*.

Only one irritating item lay in the way of a Kalamazoo victory, local voter approval of $70,000 of bonded indebtedness. A tight-fisted fiscal tradition similar to that which would earn Kalamazoo the title as "The Debt Free City" during the Great Depression had been well established by 1903 as well. The Niles *Daily Star* editor gleefully reported some residents balking at the high price under the heading "Kalamazoo has Chill." But a massive promotional campaign by the Press Club and support by both the Democrat oriented *Gazette* and the Republican *Telegraph* trumpeted the advantages of the new

Prospect Hill as it appeared prior to construction of Western Normal.

school to the city. A special election on October 19 brought an unusually large turn out of 999 voters. The bond issue passed by nearly a 9 to 1 majority.

With the ball back in its court the State Board of Education needed to select the precise site of the new normal. On a visit to Kalamazoo on November 14th the board quickly pared down the original 24 possible tracts to four. A consultant from Olmsted Brothers of Brookline, Massachusetts, the nationally famous landscape planners responsible for New York City's Central Park and the grounds of the 1893 Columbian World's Fair, visited the remaining sites and submitted a written report to the Board. Based on that recommendation the State Board decided on the property known as "Prospect Hill."

Comprising just over 20 acres that ran 1,000 feet along Davis Street to the east and bordered on the irregular contours of Asylum Avenue (now Oakland Drive) to the west, Prospect Hill presented an inauspicious appearance in 1903. Its steep sides rose to a plateau crowned by a narrow ridge 15 or 20 feet high. Abandoned pear trees and wild grape vines grew along the sides and top. Blow sand underlay a shallow layer of topsoil. Nevertheless, the Olmsteds saw potential in the neglected eminence and submitted a detailed landscape plan. Unfortunately, the state board soon discovered that to execute that plan would cost much more than the $7,500 that had been appropriated. Accordingly, the Olmsteds trimmed their grandiose plan into a no frills version.

As its representatives sought to acquire clear title to the site, money posed a problem for the City of Kalamazoo as well. Prospect Hill actually comprised two separately owned parcels and despite its unkempt appearance those owners were holding out for big money. Negotiations dragged on over three months. Nathaniel H. Stewart, president of the Kalamazoo School Board, reputedly journeyed to Massachusetts

The 39-year-old Dwight Waldo was appointed principal of Western Normal in 1904.

to appeal to one owner. At a time when Kalamazoo city lots brought $200 to $300 and surrounding farm land could be purchased for $25 to $30 an acre, the city ended up paying $24,000 for the run down twenty acre tract. On March 24, 1904, Stewart, on behalf of the citizens of Kalamazoo, presented warranty deeds for the two parcels of land to the state board. It accepted with thanks and a consideration of fifty cents for each deed.

The delay in acquiring clear title to Prospect Hill interrupted the planned building schedule. The act creating the normal had stipulated that the school building be ready for occupancy by September 1, 1904. However, not until April 16 were the bids for erection of the building opened. The Kalamazoo firm of George Rickman and Sons won the bid at $53,500 - $295 less than a Chicago company. The contract to grade and landscape the grounds was awarded to W.A. Drake of Kalamazoo on May 13th. On May 16th, almost a full year after Gov. Bliss had signed the bill, workmen using horse drawn scrapers and shovels began leveling the top of Prospect Hill. Drake's laborers drew $2 for a ten-hour work day - each team of horses earned $3.

Although the physical development of Western Normal lagged, the State Board intended to meet the June 27, 1904, formal opening date. On April 1, it appointed Dwight Bryant Waldo principal of the incipient institution. The selection of the 39-year-old administrator would prove of critical importance to the evolution of the institution.

Waldo, born in Arcade, New York, in 1864, had moved with his parents to Plainwell, Michigan, at the age of eight. He earned a bachelor's degree from Albion College in 1887 and a masters from the same institution three years later. He first taught history and economics at Beloit College and later at Albion. In 1899 he became the first principal of the newly created Northern State Normal School at Marquette. His familiarity with the area where he had grown up and his experience in pioneering the normal school at Marquette were important considerations. But it was his personality and administrative style that would leave the greatest mark.

Contemporaries remembered the moustached Waldo as a personable but stern leader who ran his institution in a paternalistic manner. He gathered information and sought advice but he alone made the decisions and rarely changed them once made. Few details concerning his institution escaped Waldo's scrutiny. In the early years he delegated but little authority, and he kept a sharp eye on student as well as faculty behavior. Loud student parties might, for example, be quickly quieted by a personal visit from the president.

Waldo treated his professors more like children than colleagues. He allowed no designations of professorial status. They were all simply teachers. He alone determined salaries, and pay increases came as a result of his own notions of efficiency rather than advanced degrees or scholarly publications. Separate scales existed for men and women teachers. He allowed academic freedom within the classroom but monitored faculty behavior and morals outside. Tobacco, for example, was barred from the campus. When Waldo learned that a teacher was practicing questionable personal morals, a summons to his office soon followed. One such culprit told Waldo "a man's off campus life should not be of any concern on the campus." The president replied that "hereafter he should spend his time exclusively off campus."

Principal Waldo (changed to president in 1908) accepted the reins of Western Normal in 1903 at a salary of $2,500 a year, the same as he had made at his post at Marquette. In addition to his administrative responsibilities Waldo would teach European and U.S.

history during the first fall term. As principal of a school that existed only on paper, Waldo's initial concern was to acquire a staff. In recruiting he demonstrated a persuasive almost hypnotic ability. Waldo knew of an efficient young woman in Vicksburg who he wanted as his secretary. He persuaded Miss Josephine Wing to leave her post as assistant postmaster there to become his only administrative assistant. Her salary would be $500 a year but would not begin until July 1. She started at once, paid her own expenses and served as registrar, publicity director, librarian, editor of the first *Western Bulletin* as well as dean of men and women the first year.

More than half of the public schools in Western Normal's territory were country schools. Waldo decided to pioneer a "rural school department" oriented toward the needs of rural educators. He choose Ernest Burnham, an old friend from Albion days, to head this unique experiment. Waldo called Burnham to Kalamazoo one Saturday, walked him to the top of desolate Prospect Hill, and explained the importance of his proposed educational mission. Waldo convinced him to leave a good job as Calhoun County school commissioner and join the embryonic normal school at a $300-a-year cut in salary.

By June 27, 1904, the opening of the first summer session at the normal, Waldo had lined up ten other instructors. Since the foundation had not even been laid for the normal building, classes were held in the Kalamazoo High School, known as the old Vine Street School. The hastily prepared catalog listed twelve departments offering a total of 78 courses. The curricula included several general teacher education degrees. Students who had graduated from the eighth grade could finish the rural school course in seven semesters. Those who sported high school diplomas could, in two years, graduate with the highest degree -

A bevy of Western Normal co-eds pose before the college's first building in 1914.

a "Life Certificate" which entitled them to teach for life in Michigan.

A total of 117 students from 13 counties enrolled for Western Normal's first session. While the scholars pursued their studies in the Vine Street School, Waldo conducted his administrative duties in the only available office space, a corner of the county school commissioner's office in the courthouse adjacent Bronson Park. Despite the inconveniences, Western's pioneer students remembered having a good time that summer. Waldo even managed to schedule six prestigious outside speakers.

Another 107 eager students arrived for the opening of Western's first regular school year on Monday September 26, 1904. Male students donned coats and ties for classroom appearances, while the coeds trailed long skirts along the city's dusty streets. With high school in session and the normal building still little more than a hole in the ground, Waldo had to secure other classroom space. A dilapidated Italianate brick building abandoned by Kalamazoo College and located north of Prospect Hill between Lovell and South streets served as an expedient.

This first regular semester included training school classes in which normal students practiced their teaching skills on Kalamazoo school children under the watchful eyes of "critic teachers." Until other facilities were readied training school classes met at the Methodist Church House and YMCA building. Not until 1909 would the training school move to its own facilities on campus. In 1911 the Normal High School (later University High) began when the eighth grade graduating class asked to continue under the normal teachers.

Despite the rather confusing nature of attending a normal without a campus, the first year of Western saw surprising progress. By October of 1904 the nucleus of the library that would surpass one million volumes by the 1980s had been established. The first shipment of books consisted entirely of psychology, educational, and reference works. By June 30, 1905, approximately 1,300 volumes stood in solemn order on the shelves.

The faculty organized a club and met at intervals to read and discuss papers on current issues. A faculty committee offered a prize of $5 to the student who could write the best school song to the tune of "The Heidelberg Stein Song." The winning entry began:

> Hail to our jolly student life,
> Hail with a right good cheer,
> Hail to our hopeful daily strife,
> To conquer without a fear.

When Waldo commented one day that the normal should have school colors, Josephine Wing cheerfully mentioned that the brown-eyed susans were in blossom. Waldo soon announced Western's colors - brown and gold.

During the first fall semester, two students who had played football in high school tried to organize a grid team for Western Normal. Fifteen of the 20 males enrolled turned out for practice but most found the sport too rough and quit. By the winter semester the pioneer basketball team played local church teams. Despite the newly adopted school yell:

> Hy-lo-zoo,
> Hy-lo-zoo,
> Western Normal Kalamazoo!

The normal team lost most of its games. The following fall, enrollment had swelled to 185 and the first Western Normal football team took the field against local high schools elevens.

Western State Normal School, Kalamazoo, Mich.

Western Normal's original building was completed in 1905.

Coach John McManus achieved a perfect record - all losses. The next year, the "Hillsmen" (Western's nickname before Broncos) tackled other college teams. In 1907, newly appointed athletic director William Spaulding's team won the state normal football championship and collegiate sports were secure at Western.

When Western Normal held its first commencement exercises on June 22, 1905, it was still a college without a campus. Eight women and one man received certificates at ceremonies held at the new Vine Street School. That pioneer class, Archibald Polley, Hebe Hunt, Vivian Simmons, Josephine La Duke, Ione Peacock, Shirley Braden, Ada Seabury, Mabel Pomeroy and Sarah Turner, dutifully listened to a commencement address on "The Larger Selfishness."

Finally, exactly one year later than mandated, Western's administrative offices moved into the completed structure atop Prospect Hill. The administration building, later renamed East Hall, presented its handsome classical facade to the citizens of Kalamazoo. An observation tower crowned the two story brick and cement temple of learning. Its 136 by 95 foot walls housed administrative offices, classrooms, a 400 seat assembly room, physics and chemistry laboratories, and the library.

Dignitaries gathered on November 23, 1905, for the formal dedication of the building and Kalamazoo turned out en masse to tour the imposing structure. Stewart, State Superintendent of Public Instruction Patrick Kelley, Governor Fred Warner and other prominent officials delivered orations. State Representative Vandercook, who became known as "The Father of Western." gave a blow by blow account of his efforts to wrestle the original bill through the legislature. Western's first historian, James Knauss, termed the occasion "one of most

Western Normal's original gymnasium shown here in 1911, now houses the University's Archives.

245

notable events in the history of Kalamazoo."

As Kalamazoo residents walked the grounds of the campus that day they might have commented on the absence of cement walks. But there was a logical reason for their delayed construction. Waldo had taken the advice of the Olmsted firm. Rather than lay out preconceived walks, Waldo would let student traffic tramp paths across the campus. Those most direct routes would then be paved.

The Administration Building, of course, was only the start of Western's physical development. Waldo campaigned hard for more building funds. In 1905, the legislature responded by appropriating $72,000 for additional construction. On June 22, 1908, dignitaries again gathered to dedicate two new structures - a gymnasium and additional classrooms adjoining the original administration building on the north.

The new gymnasium featured such avante garde luxuries as showers, a swimming pool and a baseball cage. Contemporaries described it as "one of the best planned and best equipped structures of its kind to be found in the normal schools and colleges of the Northwest Territory."

In 1909 another new structure, built to house the burgeoning training school, rose to the south of the administration building. Will Rogers would later call these classically columned structures "the Acropolis of Kalamazoo County."

As the decades passed, other buildings and property acquisitions swelled the size and complexity of the original campus. Waldo served as president of Western until 1936, when he was succeeded by Paul Sangren. As Western metamorphized from a normal to a college to a university, its enrollment would exceed 20,000 students.

Following World War II, a modern new campus sprang up across Stadium Drive and the original campus was relegated to the Business College until construction of new buildings in the 1980s and 1990s. The carefully conceived Olmsted landscaping, at one time traceable only in old postcards, would revert to a tangled thicket obscuring the majestic facades of the "Acropolis of Kalamazoo County." A campus campaign in the 1980s restored some of that lost grandure.

If you are ever fortunate enough to climb the creaking attic stairs of old East Hall to the top of the observatory, you can still get one of the best views in the city. And if you read the names and dates scribbled on the walls by generations of student visitors dating back to 1905, you may also feel some of the heritage of Western Michigan University, my alma mater.

Uncle Jake & the Sage
of East Aurora

When Elbert Hubbard stepped into his office that day in 1914 "Uncle Jake" Kindleberger thought it about the greatest thing since sliced bread - the availability of which, incidently, had been made feasible via the products of his Kalamazoo Vegetable Parchment Company.

Hubbard hailed from East Aurora, N.Y., 16 miles southwest of Buffalo, the jumping off place for the hordes of immigrants who had ridden Erie Canal boats westward in the 1820s and 1830s to start a new life in "Michigania." A flamboyant and colorful celebrity known variously as "the Sage of East Aurora" and "Fra Elbertus," Hubbard had long crusaded for simplicity and beauty in the American home. An army of artisans at his Roycroft shops in East Aurora crafted popular mission style oak furniture, hammered out copper object de art and printed and bound beautiful gift books.

Hubbard was also an opinion molder and popular philosopher who reached the American middle class through his little magazines, *The Philistine* and *Fra*, his many books and by lecturing on the Chautauqua circuit. A thorn in the side of conservative thinkers, he agitated for women's rights, more liberal divorce laws and greater marital freedom. He ridiculed formal education, lawyers, doctors and the clergy while advocating his own brand of health and salvation gospel that featured fresh air, honest toil, individualism and positive thinking.

Hubbard was also little short of a hero to Kindleberger, the guiding light behind the development of the Kalamazoo Vegetable Parchment Company (KVP) and the community of Parchment that sprang up around the plant. While Hubbard had

248

not founded East Aurora, his sprawling Roycroft operations that eventually employed 800 artisans, put it on the map. Beyond the debt owed by their respective communities, the two entrepreneurs had other traits in common. They were both self made men, crack salesmen fired by a vision of the future and they embraced the work ethic with open arms. Only one thing stood between their relationship being a match born in heaven - religion.

Kindleberger, a stern Methodist Sunday school teacher, practiced that pushy style of piety that never looses an opportunity to evangelize a lost soul. Hubbard was a free thinker and a disciple of Robert Ingersoll, "the great Agnostic." The aphorisms he coined in *The Philistine* frequently reflected his feelings about organized religion. For example, he wrote: "Othodoxy is spiritual constipation." "Man's greatest blunder has been in the trying to make peace with the skies instead of making peace with his neighbors." and "Labor is the only prayer that is ever answered."

Kindleberger decorated his paper mill with the printed mottos Hubbard had written, but needless to say, his selections ran more to the secular. Prominently displayed behind Kindleberger's desk hung Hubbard's quotations: "Push! If you can't push, pull. If you can't pull, please get out of the way." and "To Avoid Criticism. Do Nothing. Say Nothing. Be Nothing."

Criticism, it seems, had been something Hubbard rarely dodged during his fascinating career. Born in Bloomington, Illinois, in 1856, to a zealous Baptist couple who named their son Elbert Green after the two ministers who had baptized them, young Hubbard led a boyhood in which the highlight of each week featured a Calvinistic Hellfire and brimstone sermon. Subjected to a thorough religious indoctrination, Hubbard rebelled. Much to the horror

Elbert Hubbard, the Sage of East Aurora.

of his family and the community, he refused to be baptized. Those early experiences provided him with a lifelong target for his barbs of wit. He later wrote: "In most religions there is a strain of ethics, but if religion becames intense it leaves ethics out of the equation, and then you get a selfishness, a coldness, and a cruelty beyond compare."

Childhood memories of his strict father, a horseback doctor and phrenologist, inspired another of his targets - the medical profession, and quacks in particular. He wrote: Nature in her endeavors to keep men well has not only to fight disease, but often the doctor as well." and "Medical advertisements are not to let you know the disease is curable, but to make you think you have it."

Hubbard's father planned for his son to follow in his footsteps as a country practicioner, but again he rebelled. When his cousin Justin Weller, partner with John Larkin in a a soap making enterprise, offered the 16-year-old Hubbard a sales position, he jumped at the opportunity. He spent the succeeding three years hawking 20 pound boxes of soap door to door across the rural midwest. Handsome, hard working, full of good cheer and smiles and on joking terms with his customers as well as all the draymen, freight agents, hotel clerks and waitresses he encountered, Hubbard proved a crack salesman.

In 1875, when the Weller-Larken partnership dissolved, Hubbard followed Larkin to Buffalo where he established a massive soap factory. Hubbard continued to sell Larkin products and over the succeeding 14 years as the company prospered, in part due to innovative salesmanship that awarded prizes to soap buyers, Hubbard grew wealthy. In 1881 he married Bertha Crawford and three years later they bought a rambling Queene Anne house in the little village of East Aurora.

A milestone in Hubbard's intellectual

development, and one that would ultimately destroy his nuptial bliss, came in 1889 when he met Alice Moore, a young high school teacher and a "New Women," as feminists were then called. As their friendship grew Hubbard discovered in Alice a woman with ideas of her own who could provide challenging feedback to the philosophy he had developed over the years. He had found his intellectual soul mate, his "affinity," and soon their affinity turned to love.

A year later, Alice left East Aurora to attend a Boston College. And in 1892, Hubbard sold his interest in the soap company for a substantial sum and embarked on a new endeavor, concluding that "he who would excell in the realm of thought must not tarry in the domain of dollars." The following year found the 36-year-old graduate of the school of hard knocks enrolled in Harvard College. But Harvard professors found his self-confidence and popular writing style little to their liking. Hubbard lasted but three months in that ivy covered environment, an experience that embittered him and provided fodder for a lifelong battle against formal education. He later wrote: "A college degree, like a certificate of character is a good thing for those who need it" and "Now owls are not really wise - they only look that way - the owl is a sort of college professor."

While in Boston, Hubbard had visited the homes and graves of Emerson, Hawthorne and Thoreau. He decided to embark on a literary career by writing informal essays about the lives and works of the renowned literati. His very popular *Little Journeys* series, which he later expanded to include statesmen, painters, musicians, orators, philosophers, and other great men and women, would ultimately number 170 small volumes. During a research trip to Europe he met William Morris, author, poet, artist, architect, socialist, progenitor of the Arts and Crafts Movement and book maker par excellence. Morris inspired him to emulate many of his ideas about book publishing, arts and crafts design in home furnishings and benevolent paternalism in industry at the Roycroft Studios Hubbard later founded in East Aurora.

Hubbard's pleasure at the immediate success of his *Little Journey* series following his snubbing at Harvard was, no doubt, tempered by the unenviable situation he found himself in during September, 1894. That month he became the father of two daughters - Katherine born to Bertha and Miriam born to Alice. Nevertheless, he managed to keep his "affinity" a secret from his wife and following his own advice, "Get your happiness out of your work - or you'll never know what happiness is," he plunged into a frenetic period of productivity. He churned out book after popular book, launched the Roycroft industries, and widely lectured while clad in the eccentric costume and flowing locks he had adopted. By 1899, when he penned *A Message to Garcia,* of which more than 40 million copies were ultimately circulated, the sage of East Aurora had become an American popular culture phenomenon.

Even the public disclosure of his extramarital affair with Alice that emblazoned headlines in 1901 proved but a temporary setback to his prestige. The ensuing divorce and lawsuits instigated by Alice's brother in-law for child support for Miriam ultimately ended on a happier note with Hubbard's marriage to Alice. That bitter litigation, however, provided him with yet another subject for his lampoons - lawyers. He wrote: "The reason the Goddess is blindfolded is so she cannot see what the lawyers and judges do, for if she did she would fall dead."

Perhaps his greatest success lay in the little magazine he launched in 1895, *The Philistine: A Periodical of Protest.* Hubbard, as editor, wrote each monthly issue practically singlehanded. Filled with

J. KINDLEBERGER

If you come to Kalamazoo, we will show you a new building, 70 ft. x 327 ft., with basement, erected to take care of the increased business that has come to us from our advertising in THE PHILISTINE. We have orders from every corner of the globe, and at the bottom of the orders you may read : " I got your address from reading Elbert Hubbard's article concerning your plant in the June PHILISTINE." (*Signed*)

J. KINDLEBERGER

care Kalamazoo Vegetable Parchment Co., Kalamazoo, Mich.

Manufacturers of Genuine Vegetable Parchment, Wax Paper and Household Specialties

"Uncle Jake" Kindleberger posed for a 1914 *Philistine* ad.

pithy epigrams and essays on whatever he saw as a sham in society, the periodical appealed to free thinkers. It survived for 20 years and eventually boasted 200,000 subscribers.

It was research on an article about KVP that brought Hubbard to Kindleberger's office in 1914. The resulting piece, "A Palaver On Paper," appeared in the June issue of *The Philistine* What Hubbard had observed in Parchment was evidently much to his liking:

> I found the home of the Kalamazoo Vegetable Parchment Company delightfully situated on the river road, two miles north of Kalamazoo. It is an institution saturated with the spirit of mutual helpfulness and good-will. The executives are alert, able and sanguine; the employees, happy and contented and efficient. The whole place breathes the spirit of the hive - busyness, business and co-operation, activity and intelligence. A cleanliness and order prevails that mirrors the mind of the institution. For the main idea upon which the Kalamazoo Vegetable Parchment Company was formed was that of hygiene, and time and labor saving. What Lincoln was to the slave, the Kalamazoo Vegetable Parchment Company is to the housekeeper.

Whatever he had witnessed, whether Hubbard would have heaped anything but praise on the plant operated by his young admirer is open to conjecture. A friendship had blossomed between the two, despite their religious differences, and Hubbard reserved his ire for lawyers, doctors, clergymen and professors, not friends. Kindleberger's Horatio Alger-like career, also, no doubt, appealed to Hubbard as a concrete demonstration of the American dream at work.

Born in Alsace-Lorraine in 1875, Kindleberger

immigrated with his family to America at the age of ten. They eventually settled in West Carrollton, Ohio, where Kindleberger's father found work at a paper factory. Hardship and poverty were young Kindleberger's lot in Ohio. At the age of ten he went to work full time as a rag sorter in the paper mill to help feed his five siblings. Each ten hour work day netted him 25 cents. Worse yet, his vision was so poor that he could find the buttons he was required to remove from the rags only by touch. After work he walked the railroad tracks gathering stray chunks of coal to keep the family from freezing.

Kindleberger won promotion to "hand" on a paper machine and a raise in pay when he was 13. But he best remembered that job as "years spent dodging the heavy boot of the foreman." Two years later came an experience that would change his life. He and a gang of young mill hoodlums went to a Methodist revival meeting to have a little fun heckling. But the "sky pilot" spoke so elequently that Kindleberger saw the light. Converted and befriended by church members, Kindleberger received his first formal education by learning to read the bible. But learning came hard due to his weak eyesight. Not until he was 19 would a church member give him his first pair of glasses. He later remembered: "I sobbed when I first saw it all. I hadn't dreamed there was so much beauty. For days I just wandered about, drinking in the loveliness of the earth."

The myopic Methodist set his sights on becoming a minister. He enrolled in nearby Ohio Wesleyan University, paying his way by selling door to door. As he hawked books, hat racks, steam cookers and other gadgets he found he had a knack for salesmanship. But during his third year of studies his overworked eyes gave out on him. A doctor told him if he continued in college the strain would render him totally blind.

Proud of the cleanliness of its plant, KVP held a banquet in a "stoke hole" in the 1920s.

So Kindleberger relinquished his pulpit asperations and took to the road selling fireless cookers full time. He grew more and more adept at talking housewives into buying something they never thought they needed until he knocked on their door, eventually earning $100 a week during an era when most factory workers counted themselves fortunate to take home $10 or $11 in their pay envelopes.

In 1897, Kindleberger returned to the West Carrollton paper company as a salesman because he thought selling paper held more potential. He was right. With a sales territory that included the entire North American continent, he became "one of the best salesmen the paper industry has ever known." Soon his commissions brought him $500 a month.

During the succeeding 13 years, Kindleberger came under the sway of the sage of East Aurora. When in the vicinity, he stopped off at the Roycroft Inn which had become an intellectual mecca for increasing numbers of Americans including: Theodore Roosevelt, Booker T. Washington, Clarence Darrow and Henry Ford. There he chatted with Fra Elbertus, and the two master salesmen soon developed a firm rapport.

In 1909 Kindleberger and his brother-in-law, Harry Zimmerman, decided the time was ripe for the launching of a paper making venture of their own. They convinced a number of investors from Kalamazoo, then the nation's leading producer of paper, to finance a plant specializing in vegetable parchment, a water resistant product made by applying sulfuric acid to paper. Under adverse conditions, Kindleberger, Zimmerman and a pioneer work force of 15 employees spent the winter of 1909-1910 converting a former sugar beet factory located on the bank of the Kalamazoo River north of the city and installng equipment. Production at KVP began in April, 1910, and the following year a machine for

Kindleberger and others posed in the Parchment Community House at Christmas in 1926.

waxing paper was added.

Kindleberger, whose first official title was salesman, emerged as the dominent force behind the venture. Yet despite his hard work and drive, sales of KVP products, including bread wrappers, waxed food containers and kitchen aids, did not really take off until Hubbard's 1914 visit and the national publicity generated by his ebullient article in *The Philistine*. That coup gave Kindleberger additional insight as to what "printed salesmanship" could do and he utilized techniques such as sales letters and his own little magazines *The Parchment Prattler* and the *KVP Philosopher*, ala *The Philistine*, to gain parchment converts from coast to coast. Business boomed for KVP, the plant expanded into paper production and package printing while more and more employees built houses on lots offered cheaply in the company town called Parchment.

The June, 1914, issue of *The Philistine* that gave KVP its boost contained another of Hubbard's epigrams that proved prophetic -"Peace: An interesting interval between fights." Two months later Europe was at war.

In the spring of 1915 Hubbard decided to go to Europe and in the ex officio role he had adopted, "Inspector of the Universe," carry a personal peace message to German officials. Alice and he booked passage on the *Lusitania*. Their's were among the 1,198 lives lost when a German U-boat torpedoed the British steamer without warning off the coast of Ireland on May 7.

Elbert Hubbard II, known as Bert, carried on his father's work at East Aurora and the Roycroft shops continued to turn out hammered copper implements and millions of publications through the early years of the Depression. In 1927, Hubbard II visited Parchment and wrote a "Little Journey," *The Story of KVP*. He retained his father's flair for words and his enthusism for Parchment. He wrote:

A little village known as Parchment nestles in the crook of the river's arm and picturesque bungalows peep at one through bowers of roses. Modern and convenient homes surrounded by spacious lawns and delightful gardens fringe the bowered road and a well-equipped school building provides for the children exceptionally fine educational advantages. The community idea is strong and is encouraged in every way by the K.V.P. officials and executives who themselves work and laugh and play with their co-workers. A spacious Community House serves as a civic center. A gymnasium, auditorium, cafeteria, dining room and kitchen meet the requirements of social gatherings and entertainments. An orchestra, a band, a glee club, boy scout and campfire girls, with other societies and organizations are some of the active agents that go to make up the citizenry of Parchment. And last, but by no means least, the spiritual food necessary to a robust and fully-rounded manhood and womanhood is provided by a Sunday School and undenominational religious services held regularly therein. The K.V.P. Mills themselves stand in a one-hundred-fifty acre park. They employ eight hundred men and women - clean, healthy folks, all of them. They have to be. Every K.V.P. helper is given a thorough medical examination. As Mr. Kindleberger said, "Paper is so closely allied with our bread and butter and the things we eat that it can not be made of too clean materials, by too clean methods and processes, or by too clean men and women. Our helpers must be free from disease and on friendly terms with soap and water." And I noticed as I made a little journey through the mills that his super cleanlines ideal was rigidly upheld.

By the Depression era the KVP plants stretched for nearly a mile along the Kalamazoo River.

Kindleberger continued to present copies of Hubbard books to business associates and employees at Christmas and periodically he redecorated the plant with additional Hubbard epigrams about loyalty, quality and the value of hard work.

By the early 1930s KVP employed 1,300 people and its plants stretched for nearly a mile along the Kalamazoo River. Parchment became a village in 1930 and received a city charter nine years later. During the bleak years of the early Depression, Kindleberger donated a hilly 38-acre tract to Parchment and kept employees at work during slack times converting it into a park. Taxes remained low in the "model city" because KVP provided water service, street maintenance and fire protection. Uncle Jake, as he like to be called, also practiced a paternal supervision over the community, personally insuring that employee's morals, and their homes and lawns, were maintained on a par with his own high standards. The Community House where Uncle Jake sometimes delivered sermons and taught Sunday school served as the center of Parchment's social life.

Whether or not a peccadillo in 1931 that resulted in Kindleberger coming out on the loosing end of a several thousand dollar swindle perpetrated by bunco artist Yellow Kid Weil proves the old adage "you can't con an honest man" had best be left unanswered. Perhaps one of Kindleberger's favorite Hubbard mottos included in the memorial issue of the KVP *Philosopher* following his death in 1947 says it best: "Blessed is the man who does not bellyache."

Today, the city Uncle Jake founded remains rightfully proud of its Kindleberger Park and residents of East Aurora enjoy their Hubbard Park, fitting memorials to two master salesmen.

SOURCES

Drama in the Dunes

Dunbar, Willis. *Michigan A History of the Wolverine State.* Grand Rapids, [1980].

(Durant, Samuel) *History of Kalamazoo County, Michigan.* Philadelphia, 1880.

Hayes, A.A. "The Metropolis of the Prairies." *Harper's New Monthly Magazine.* October, 1880. p. 711.

Hodge, Frederick Webb, ed. *Handbook of American Indians North of Mexico.* 2 Vols. Washington, 1912.

Hubbard, Gurdon S. *The Autobiography of.* Chicago, 1911.

Hubbard, Gurdon S. "Incidents in the Administration of Indian Justice," *Michigan Pioneer Collections.* Vol. 3 (1881) p. 127.

Kinietz, W. Vernon. *The Indians of the Western Great Lakes 1615-1760.* Ann Arbor, 1940.

McClurken, James M. *Gah-Baeh-Jhagwah-Buk. The Way It Happened.* East Lansing, (1991).

Porter, Phil. *View From the Veranda: The History and Architecture of the Summer Cottages on Mackinac Island.* Mackinac Island, 1981.

Voyageur Vittles

Anderson, Thomas G. "Narative of..." *Wisconsin Historical Collections.* Vol. IX, (1882). p. 137.

Ballantyne, Robert Michael. *Hudson Bay; or Everyday Life in the Wilds of North America.* London, 1879.

Blegen, Theodore C. *The Voyageurs and Their Songs.* St. Paul, Minn., 1966.

Gates, Charles M., ed. *Five Fur Traders of the Northwest.* St. Paul, Minn., 1933.

[Gilman, Chandler Robbins]. *Life on the Lakes...* 2 Vols. New York, 1836.

Hamilton, H.E., ed. *Incidents and Events in the Life of Gurdon Hubbard.* Chicago, 1888.

Hubbard, Bela. "The Early Colonization of Detroit," *Michigan Pioneer Collections.* Vol. 1 (1877). p. 347.

McKenney, Thomas L. *Sketches of a Tour to the Lakes...* Baltimore, 1827.

Masson, L.R. *Les Bourgeois De La Compagnie du Nord Quest...* 2 Vols. Quebec, 1889.

Nute, Grace Lee. *The Voyageur.* New York, 1931.

Young, Edgerton Ryerson. *Stories from Indian Wigwams and*

Northern Camp-Fires. New York, 1893.

Mackinac Memories

Agassiz, Louis and Cabot, J. Elliot. *Lake Superior, its Physical Character, Vegetation and Animals.* Boston, 1850.

Baxter, James Phinney, ed. *The Pioneers of New France in New England, with Contemporary Letters and Documents.* Albany, 1894.

Beaven, James. *Recreations of a Long Vacation; or a Visit to Indian Missions in Upper Canada.* London, 1846.

Bigsby, John J. *The Shoe and Canoe or Pictures of Travel in the Canadas...* 2 Vols. London, 1850.

Blackbird, Andrew. *History of the Ottawa and Chippewa Indians of Michigan...* Ypsilanti, 1887.

Bryant, William Cullen, *Letters of a Traveller...* New York, 1850.

Butterfield, Consul W. *History of the Discovery of the Northwest by John Nicolet...* Cincinnati, 1881.

Carter, James L. and Rankin, Ernest H., eds. *North to Lake Superior: The Journal of Charles W. Penny 1840.* Marquette., 1970.

Carver, Jonathan. *Travels Through the Interior Parts of North America... 1766-68.* London, 1778.

Charlevoix, Pierre Francois-Xavier. *A Voyage to North America...* 2 Vols. Dublin, 1766.

Colton, Calvin. *Tour of the American Lakes, and Among the Indians of the North-West Territory in 1830...* 2 Vols. London, 1833.

Disturnell, John, compiler, *The Great Lakes or Inland Seas of America.* New York, 1863.

_____. *Island of Mackinac...* Philadelphia, 1875.

_____. compiler. *Springs, Water-Falls, Sea Baths, Resorts, and Mountain Scenery of the United States and Canada...* New York, 1855.

_____. compiler. *A Trip Through the Lakes of North America.* New York, 1857.

Dunbar, Willis F. *Michigan: A History of the Wolverine State.* Revised Edition. Grand Rapids, [1980].

Featherstonhaugh, G.W. *A Canoe Voyage up the Minnay Sotor...* London, 1847.

[Gilman, Chandler R.] *Life on the Lakes; Being Tales and Sketches Collected During a Trip to the Pictured Rocks of Lake Superior.* 2 Vols. New York, 1836.

Hamilton, H.E., ed. *Incidents and Events in the Life of Gurdon Hubbard.* Chicago, 1888.

Hammond, John Martin. *Quaint and Historic Forts of North America*. Philadelphia, 1915.

Havighurst, Walter. *Three Flags at the Straits: The Forts of Mackinac*. Englewood Cliffs, N.J., [1966].

Hennepin, Louis. *A New Discovery of a Vast Country in America*. Reprinted with editing by Reuben Gold Thwaites. 2 Vols. Chicago,1903.

Henry, Alexander. *Travels and Adventures in Canada and the Indian Territories Between the Years 1760 and 1776*. New York, 1809.

Heriot, George. *Travels Throught the Canadas...* Philadelphia, 1813.

Howes, Wright. *U.S. Iana*. New York, 1962.

Huback, Robert R. *Early Midwestern Travel Narratives: An Annotated Bibliography 1634-1850*. Detroit, 1961.

Hubbard, Bela. *Memorials of A Half-Century in Michigan and the Lake Region*. New York, 1887.

Jameson, Anna. *Winter Studies and Summer Rambles in Canada*. 2 Vols. New York, 1839.

Kane, Paul. *Wanderings of an Artist Among the Indians of North America...* London, 1859.

Lahontan, Baron de. *New Voyages to North America*. Reprinted with editing by Reuben Gold Thwaites. 2 Vols. Chicago, 1905.

Lanman, Charles. *Haw-Ho-Noo; or Records of a Tourist*. Philadelphia, 1850.

Logan, James. *Notes of Journey Through Canada, the United States of America, and the West Indies*. Edinburgh, 1838.

Long, John. *Voyages and Travels of an Indian Interpreter and Trader...* London, 1791.

McElroy, Robert and Riggs, Thomas, eds. *The Unfortified Boundary: A Diary of the First Survey of the Canadian Boundary Line... by Major Joseph Delafield...* New York, 1943.

McKenney, Thomas L. *Sketches of a Tour to the Lakes...* Baltimore, 1827.

Mackinac Island (View Book). New York, 1886.

Mansfield, Edward D. *Exposition of the Natural Positon of Mackinaw City...* Cincinnati, 1857.

Marryat, Frederick. *A Diary in America with Remarks on its Institutions*. New York, 1839.

Martineau, Harriet. *Society in America*. 2 Vols. Paris, 1837.

Massie, Larry B. "The Literature of the Mackinac Country," introduction to Williams, Meade C. *Early Mackinac*. AuTrain, 1987.

Myer, Jesse S. *Life and Letters of Dr. William Beaumont*. St. Louis, 1912.

Northrup, A. Judd. *Camps and Tramps in the Adirondacks and Grayling Fishing in Northern Michigan*. Syracuse, N.Y., 1880.

Pitezel, John H. *Lights and Shades of Missionary LIfe...* Cincinnati, 1859.

Porter, Mary H. *Eliza Chappell Porter: A Memoir*. Chicago, [1892].

Quaife, Milo, ed. *The John Askin Papers*. 2 Vols. Detroit, 1928, 1931.

_____. ed. *The Western Country in the 17th Century: The Memoirs of Lamothe Cadillac and Pierre Liette*. Chicago, 1947.

Rogers, Robert. *A Concise Account of North America...* London. 1765.

Romig, Walter. *Michigan Place Names*. Detroit, 1986.

Schoolcraft, Henry Rowe. *Narrative Journal of Travels Through the Northwestern Regions of the United States...* Albany, 1821

Shea, John Gilmary, ed. *Discovery and Exploration of the Mississippi Valley: with the Original Narratives of Marquette...* New York, 1852.

_____. ed. *A Discription of Louisiana, by Father Louis Hennepin...* New York, 1880.

Standard Guide Mackinac Island and Northern Lake Resorts. N.P., 1899.

Strickland, W.F. *Old Mackinaw; or, the Fortress of the Lakes...* Philadelphia, 1860.

Stuart Letters of Robert and Elizabeth Sullivan Stuart and their Children 1819-1864... 2 Vols. Privately Printed, 1961.

Van Fleet, J.A. *Old and New Mackinac...* Ann Arbor, 1870.

_____. *Summer Resorts of the Mackinaw Region*. Detroit, 1882.

Weed, Thurlow. "A Half Century Ago" in Mansfield, J.B., compiler. *History of the Great Lakes*. 2 Vols. Chicago, 1899.

Williams, Mead C. *Early Mackinac: "The Fairy Island."* St. Louis, [1897].

Wilson, James Grant and Fiske, John, eds. *Appleton's Cyclopedia of American Biography*. 6 Vols. New York, 1888.

Wood, Edwin O. *Historic Mackinac*. 2 Vols. New York, 1918.

Woolson, Constance F. "Round By Propellor," *Harper's New*

Monthly Magazine. September, 1872. p. 518.

Depot Schemes

Barnett, LeRoy. *Railroads in Michigan A Catalog of Company Publications 1836-1980.* Marquette, 1986.

Blair, Walter, ed. *The Sweet Singer of Michigan.* Chicago, 1928.

Bullinger, Edwin W., compiler. *Postal and Shippers Guide for the United States and Canada.* New York, 1893.

Busbey, T. Addison, ed. *Biographical Directory of the Railroad Officials of America.* 1901 edition. Chicago, [1901].

Dillenback [J.D.] & Leavitt. *History and Directory of Kent County, Michigan.* Grand Rapids, 1870.

Dunbar, Willis F. *All Aboard! A History of Railroads in Michigan.* Grand Rapids, [1969].

Greenly, A.H. "The Sweet Singer of Michigan Bibliographically Considered," *The Papers of the Bibliographical Society of America.* Vol. 39 No. 2 [1945].

Hartwick L.M. & Tuller, W.H. *Oceana County Pioneers and Business Men of Today.* Pentwater, 1890.

History of Kent County, Michigan. Chicago, 1881.

[Kitching, J.W.] *Tales of Rudyard As Told By the Folks.* [Rudyard, 1922].

Meints, Graydon M. *Along the Tracks: A Directory of Named Places on Michigan Railroads.* Mount Pleasant, 1987.

_____. *Michigan Railroads & Railroad Companies.* East Lansing, 1992.

Michigan: A Guide to the Wolverine State. New York, [1941].

Michigan Biographies. 2 Vols. Lansing, 1924.

Michigan Manual. Lansing, 1880-1898.

Report of the Commissioner of Railroads. Lansing, 1877-1900.

Rogers, Howard S. *History of Cass County.* Cassopolis, 1875.

Romig, Walter. *Michigan Place Names.* Detroit, 1986.

Laurence of Superior

Agassiz, Louis and Cabot, J. Elliot. *Lake Superior, its Physical Character, Vegetation and Animals.* Boston, 1850.

Andreas, A.T. *History of the Upper Peninsula of Michigan.* Chicago, 1883.

Bayliss, Joseph E. and Estelle L. and Quaife, Milo M. *River of Destiny: The Saint Marys.* Detroit, 1955.

Harper's Weekly. 5 January 1889. p. 5 & 7.

Langer, William L., ed. *An Encyclopedia of World History.* Boston, 1968.

Lee, Sidney, ed. *Dictionary of National Biography*, Vol. 14. New York, 1909.

Mansfield, J.B., ed. *History of the Great Lakes.* 2 Vols. Chicago, 1899.

Marquette, Michigan, Illustrated... Marquette, 1891.

Moore, Charles F., compiler. *The St. Marys Falls Canal Exercises at the Semi-Centennial Celebration...* Detroit, 1907.

Morris, Richard B. *Encyclopedia of American History.* New York, [1953].

Newton, Stanley. *The Story of Sault Ste. Marie and Chippewa County.* Sault Ste. Marie, 1923.

Oliphant, Lawrence. *Minnesota and the Far West.* Edinburgh and London, 1855.

[Osborne, Chase S.] *The "Soo" Scenes in and About Sault Ste. Marie.* [Milwaukee, 1887].

Seldes, Gilbert. *The Stammering Century.* New York, [1928].

Wolff, Julius F. *Lake Superior Shipwrecks.* [Duluth, 1990].

Celery City Quacks

Annual Reports of the City of Kalamazoo. Kalamzoo, 1890-1900.

Burr, C.B., ed. *Medical History of Michigan.* 2 Vols. Minneapolis, 1930.

Cramp, Arthur J., ed. *Nostrums and Quackery.* 3 Vols. Chicago, 1911, 1921, 1936.

Dunbar, Willis. *Kalamazoo and How It Grew... and Grew.* Kalamazoo, 1969.

"Greater Kalamazoo." Supplement to Kalamazoo *Daily Gazette.* 30 July 1904.

Hiss, A. Emil. *The Standard Manual of Soda and Other Beverages.* Chicago, 1902.

Holbrook, Stewart H. *The Golden Age of Quackery.* New York, 1959.

Kalamazoo City Directory. Kalamazoo 1860-1930. Title and Publishers vary.

Kalamazoo Gazette. 1895-1902.

Lilly's Handboook of Pharmacy and Therapeutics. Indianapolis, 1898.

Lloyd, John U. *Elixirs Their History, Formula and Methods of Preparation.* Cincinnati, 1883.

McNair, Rush. *Medical Memories of 50 years in Kalamazoo.* N.P., [1938].

Massie, Larry B. and Schmitt, Peter. *Kalamazoo: The Place Behind the Products.* [Woodland Hills, Ca., 1981].

Morrill, S.E. *A Treatise of Practical Instructions in the Medical and Surgical Uses of Electricity.* Kalamazoo, 1882.

Yonkerman Consumption Remedy Company. *Consumption: Its Diagnosis, Treatment and Cure.* Kalamazoo, [ca. 1905].

Young, James Harvey. *The Toadstool Millionaires.* Princeton, N.J., 1961.

Zoa-Phora Medicine Company. *Advice to Mothers Concerning Diseases of Women and Children...* Kalamazoo, 1885.

Literary Lumberjacks

Anderson, Julie. *I Married A Logger; Life in Michigan's Tall Timber.* New York, [1951].

Andrews, Clarence A. *Michigan in Literature.* Detroit, (1992).

Beck, Earl C. *Lore of the Lumber Camps.* Ann Arbor, 1948.

Belding, George Angus. *Tales From the Presque Isle Woods.* New York, [1946].

Benson, Barbara E. *Logs and Lumber: The Development of Lumbering in Michigan's Lower Peninsula 1837-1870.* Mt. Pleasant, 1989.

Black, Albert. *Michigan Novels: An Annotated Bibliography.* (Ann Arbor, 1963).

Blakeman, Charles E. *Report of a Truant: A True Story.* [Grand Rapids, 1928].

Corrigan, George A. *Calked Boots and Cant Hooks.* [Park Falls, Wis., 1976].

Covert, William Chalmers. *Glory of the Pines.* Philadelphia, 1914.

Dollar, Robert. *Memoirs of.* 3rd Ed. San Francisco, 1927.

Dorson, Richard M. *Bloodstoppers and Bearwalkers: Folk Traditions of the Upper Peninsula.* Cambridge, 1952.

Fitzmaurice, John W. *The Shanty Boy, or Life in a Lumber Camp...* Cheboygan, 1889.

Foehl, Harold M. and Hargreaves, Irene M. *The Story of Logging the White Pine in the Saginaw Valley.* Bay City, [1964].

Goodrich, Madge Knevels. *A Bibliography of Michigan Authors.* Richmond, Va., 1928.

Greenly, Albert Harry. *A Selective Bibliography of Important Books, Pamphlets and Broadsides Relating to Michigan History.* Lunenburg, Vt., 1958.

Holbrook, Stewart H. *Holy Old Mackinaw: A Natural History of the American Lumberjack.* New York, 1938.

Hotchkiss, George W. *History of the Lumber and Forest Industry of the Northwest.* Chicago, 1898.

_____. *Industrial Chicago: The Lumber Interests.* Chicago, 1894.

Hurlbert, William D. *White Pine Days on the Tahquamenon.* Lansing, 1949.

Karamanski, Theodore. *Deep Woods Frontier: A History of Logging in Northern Michigan.* Detroit, 1989.

Kilar, Jeremy W. *Michigan Lumbertowns: Lumbermen and Laborers in Saginaw, Bay City and Muskegon 1870-1905.*Detroit, 1990.

Kunitz, Stanley J. and Haycraft, Howard. *Twentieth Century Authors.* N.Y., 1942.

Kunitz, Stanley J. and Colby, Vineta. *Twentieth Century Authors.* First Supplement. N.Y., 1955.

Lewis, George Edward. *Heart Echoes.* Grand Rapids, [1899].

[Lewis, George Edward]. *Jim.* [Grand Rapids, 1909].

_____. *Nick of the Woods.* Portland, Oregon, 1916.

Mallock, Douglas. *Tote Road and Trail.* Indianapolis, [1917].

Marinette and Menominee Illustrated and Described. Art Publishing Company, Pratt and Owen, 1887.

Maybee, Rolland H. *Michigan's White Pine Era 1840-1900.* Lansing, 1960.

Mosher, Edith R. and Williams, Nella Dietrich. *From Indian Legends to the Modern Book-Shelf.* Ann Arbor, 1931.

Nelligan, John Emmett and Sheridan, Charles M. *The Life of a Lumberman.* N.P., [1929].

Newton, Stan. *Paul Bunyan of the Great Lakes.* Chicago, [1946].

Overton, Grant. *When Winter Comes to Main Streeet.* New York, [1922].

Powers, Kate Ball, Hopkins, Flora Ball and Ball, Lucy, compilers. *Autobiography of John Ball.* Grand Rapids, 1925.

Puddefoot, William G. *Leaves from the Log of a Sky Pilot.* Boston, [1915].

_____. *The Minute Man on the Frontier.* New York, [1895].

_____. & Rankin, Isaac. *Hewers of Wood: A Story of the Michigan Pine Forests.* Boston, [1903].

Reiman, Lewis C. *Between the Iron and the Pine.* [Ann Arbor, 1951].

_____. *Incredible Seney.* [Ann Arbor, 1953].

_____. *When Pine Was King*. [Ann Arbor, 1952].

Rickaby, Franz. *Ballads and Songs of the Shanty-Boy*. Cambridge, 1926.

Romig, Walter. *Michigan Place Names*. Detroit, 1986.

Russell, Curran N. and Baer, Donna Degen. *The Lumbermen's Legacy*. Manistee, 1954.

Skinner, George Wallace. *The Axe Thrower of the Tittabawassee*. Weidman, MI., 1935.

Smallwood, Carol, ed. *Michigan Authors*. Hillsdale, 1993.

Sorden, L.G. *Lumberjack Lingo*. Spring Green, Wis., [1969].

Stephenson, Isaac. *Recollections of a Long Life: 1829-1915*. Chicago, 1915.

Stevens, James. *The Saginaw Paul Bunyan*. New York, 1932.

White, Stewart Edward. *The Riverman*. New York, 1908.

Stoves

Beasley, Norman and Stark, George W. *Made in Detroit*. New York, [1957].

Catlin, George B. *The Story of Detroit*. Detroit, 1926.

Craig, Sarah E. *Scientific Cooking with Scientific Methods*. Battle Creek, [1911].

Dunbar, Willis F. *Michigan: A History of the Wolverine State*. Grand Rapids., 1980.

Farmer, Silas. *History of Detroit and Wayne County...* 2 Vols. 3rd. Ed. Detroit, 1890.

"From Factory to Family at Factory Prices." Kalamazoo Stove Company Catalog. 1933.

Glover, Lowell H. *A Twentieth Century History of Cass County, Michigan*. Chicago, 1906.

Gregory, Michael L. *The Forgotten Years of Battle Creek*. Galesburg, [ca. 1987].

Hyma, Albert. *Albertus Van Raalte and His Dutch Settlements in the United States*. Grand Rapids, 1947.

Massie Larry B. *The Holland Area: Warm Friends and Wooden Shoes*. [Woodland Hills, CA., 1988].

_____.and Schmitt, Peter. *Kalamazoo: The Place Behind the Products*. [Woodland Hills, CA,1981].

Michigan Department of Labor, Annual Report. Lansing, 1902, 1905, 1917.

Vandenburg, Berenice E. *A Dowagiac Collection*. Berrien Springs, [1982].

Custer, Glazier and Paul Revere

American Biographical History of Eminent and Self-Made Men. Michigan Volume. Cincinnati, 1878.

Ceremonies Attending the Unveiling of the Equestrian Statue to Major General George Armstrong Custer... N.D., (1910).

Faust, Patricia L., ed. *Historical Times Illustrated Encyclodpedia of the Civil War.* New York, (1986).

Glazier, Willard. *The Capture, the Prison Pen, and the Escape...* New York, 1868.

_____. *Ocean to Ocean on Horseback.* Philadelphia, 1896.

Owens, John A. *Sword and Pen...* Philadelphia, 1880.

Robertson, John. *Michigan in the War.* Lansing, 1882.

Wilson, James G. & Fiske, John, eds. *Appleton's Cyclopedia of American Biography.* 6 Vols. N.Y., 1888.

Corsets

Cotton, Martha. "16 Corset-making Companies Shaped Economy Here in 1900," *Jackson Citizen Patriot.* 18 March 1987. p. BB-10.

Jackson Daily Citizen. Industrial Edition. 1889.

Hagar, Dave. "Women Led this 1912 Labor Battle in Kalmazoo," *Kalamazoo Gazette.* 19 Sept. 1982.

"The Manufacture of Ladies' Corsets," *Twenty-fifth Annual Report of the Michigan Bureau of Labor and Industrial Statistics...* Lansing, 1908. p. 468.

Massie, Larry B. and Schmitt, Peter. *Battle Creek: The Place Behind the Products.* [Woodland Hills, CA. 1984].

_____. & _____. *Kalamazoo: The Place Behind the Products.* [Woodland Hills, CA., 1981].

Report of the Michigan State Commission of Inquiry into Wages and Conditions of Labor for Women... Lansing, 1915.

Acropolis of Kalamazoo

Appledoorn, Fred. *Transcript of Oral Interview* conducted by John Yzenbaard on 23 June 1964.

Brown and Gold (Western Normal Year Book). 1911, 1914.

Cleaver, Carol H. "Local Woman Once Carried Original Plans of WMU in Coat Pocket," *Kalamazoo Gazette.* 1 Nov. 1959.

Dunbar, Willis F. *The Michigan Record in Higher Education.* Detroit, 1963.

Knauss, James O. *The First Fifty Years: A History of Western Michigan College of Education 1903-1953.* Kalamazoo, 1953.

_____. Knauss, James O. *History of Western State*

273

Teachers College 1904-1929. Kalamazoo, [1929].

Niles Daily Star. 31 Aug. 1903 p. 3, and 1 Sept. 1903, p. 4.

Stine, Leo. C. *Western - A Twentieth Century University.* Kalamazoo, [1980].

Twenty Years 1904-1924. Kalamazoo, 1924.

Uncle Jake and the Sage of East Aurora

Balch, David Arnold. *Elbert Hubbard Genius of Roycroft.* New York, 1940.

Champney, Freeman. *Art and Glory: The Story of Elbert Hubbard.* New York, [1968].

Hamilton, Charles F. *As Bees In Honey Drown: Elbert Hubbard and the Roycrofters.* [Cranbury, N.J., 1973].

[Hubbard, Elbert]. *The Roycroft Dictionary.* East Aurora, New York, 1914.

Kindleberger, Jacob. "History of K.V.P.", manuscript. at Parchment Public Library.

Massie, Larry B. and Schmitt, Peter. *Kalamazoo: The Place Behind the Products.* [Woodland HIlls, CA., 1981].

Parchment 1939-1989. Supplement to Kalamazoo Gazette. 12 July 1989.

The Philistine. June, 1914.

Shay, Felix. *Albert Hubbard of East Aurora.* New York, 1926.

Stewart, Glenn., ed. *KVP Philosopher.* Vol. 16, No. 2. February, 1947.

The Story of K.V.P. East Aurora, N.Y., 1927.

Bruce, James 113
Bryant, William C. 88
Buchanan 217
Buckland Mills, VA. 208
Buffalo 50, 69, 88, 248, 251
Burnham, Ernest 239
Burt, Henriette 110
Burtt, William 197
Bush, James L. 110

Cabot, J. Elliot 89, 116
Cadillac 159, 160
Cadillac, Antoine 17, 53, 55
Calkins, Elias B. 110
Calkinsville 110,111
Cape Town, South Africa 112
Carland 109
Carver, Jonathan 58, 60
Cass County 197
Cass, Lewis 66, 72, 185
Catherwood, Mary H. 93
Celery Medicine Co. 137, 138
Central State Normal 231
Chadwick 107
Chapel, Eliza 73, 74
Charleston, S.C. 208
Charlevoix, Pierre 55, 56
Cheeseborough, Nicholas 104
Chelsea 211
Cheseboro, Nathaniel 104
Cheyenne, WY. 217
Chicago 14, 16, 26, 74, 82, 88, 127, 180, 191, 226
Chicago & Northwestern R.R. 98, 100, 104, 107
Chicago & West Michigan R.R. 94, 106 107, 110
Chippewa County 95, 100, 177
Chippewa House 115-117
Chippewa Tribe 16, 56, 61, 82, 84, 85, 120
Cincinnati 44
Civil War 205-219
Clare County 100, 106, 110

Cleveland, OH. 205
Cliff Mine 126
Colman 109
Colman, Howard G. 140
Colton, Calvin 73
Columbia, S.C. 208
Comstock 214
Comus 100
Cook, Madame 149
Cooper, Benjamin F. 109
Coopersville 109
Copper Harbor 125
Coronet Corset Co. 224
Corrigan, George A. 169, 170
Covert, William C. 175
Crawford, Bertha 251
Crawford County 101, 106
Crimean War 127
Croghan, George 65, 72
Crooked Lake 100
Crooks, Ramsay 16, 66
Curtenius, Frederick 213
Custer, George A. 205-219
Custer, Libbie 210, 211, 219
Custer Monument Assoc. 210, 219

Dablon, Claude 49
Danville, GA. 208
Darby, George L. 214
Darrow, Clarence 258
Day River 98
Dearborn 188
Decatur 101, 214, 216, 217, 231
De Graff, Harmon 195
Delafield, Joseph 66, 67
Delta County 97, 98, 107
Deschamps, - 16
Detroit 55, 56, 60, 62, 67, 69, 73, 74, 76-78, 80, 84, 94, 193-197, 199, 204, 211, 222, 228
Detroit & Bay City R.R. 103
Detroit, Grand Haven & Milwaukee R.R. 101, 109

Larry B. Massie is a Michigan product and proud of it. Born in Grand Rapids in 1947, he grew up in Allegan. Following a tour in Viet Nam as a U. S. Army paratrooper, he worked as a telephone lineman, construction laborer, bartender and in a pickle factory before earning three degrees in history from Western Michigan University.

He honed his research skills during an eight-year position with the W. M. U. Archives and Regional History Collection. He left in 1983 to launch a career as a freelance historian, specializing in the heritage of the state he loves. An avid book collector, he lives with his wife and workmate Priscilla, and their 35, 000 volume library, in a rambling old schoolhouse nestled in the Allegan State Forest. Sons Adam, Wallie, Larry Jr. and daughter Maureen, insure there is never a dull moment.

Larry B. Massie and the new deluxe edition.

Larry and Priscilla Massie's

MICHIGAN HISTORY BOOKS AVAILABLE FROM THE
PRISCILLA PRESS

Michigan Memories   288 pages, ill. bib. index. $10.95

Birchbark Belles   310 pages, ill. bib. index. $10.95

Potawatomi Tears and Petticoat Pioneers 296 pages, ill. bib. index.
$8.95

The Romance of Michigan's Past 270 pages, ill. bib. index. $8.95

Pig Boats and River Hogs 296 pages, ill. bib. index. $8.95

Copper Trails and Iron Rails 290 pages, ill. bib. index. $10.95

Voyages into Michigan's Past 298 pages, ill. bib. index. $10.95

Walnut Pickles and Watermelon Cake: A Century of Michigan
Cookery 354 pages, 8 1/2 x 11, ill. bib. index, hardbound. $24.95

Warm Friends and Wooden Shoes: An Illustrated History of
Holland, Michigan 128 pages, 8 1/2 x 11, ill. bib. index, hardbound.
$19.95

Shipping on individual books $1.50
Two or more books ordered retail—shipping is free
Michigan residents please add 6% sales tax

Order from Priscilla Massie
2109 41ST STREET
ALLEGAN FOREST, MICHIGAN 49010
(616) 673-3633

Please indicate if you would like the author to inscribe the books.

287

DATE DUE

FEB 22			